WHEN IN
DOUBT
CALL 91:1

When In Doubt, CALL 91:1
By: Rhonece Ford

Copyright © 2025 Rhonece Ford

(Second Edition)
Published by: HigherLife Publishing

ISBN: 978-1-964081-30-4 Paperback
ISBN: 9781964081335 eBook

Independently published

Library of Congress Control Number: 1-14812141621

WHEN IN DOUBT CALL 91:1

He that dwelleth in the secret place of the most High shall abide under the shadow of the Almighty.

Rhonece Ford

TESTIMONY

This book was inspired during a time in my life when I felt heavy. I was mad with God and made a decision to start my life over in another state. The day after moving into my college apartment I spent two weeks in a nearby hospital trying to recover from a T-bone car accident. The exact place where I started to resent God, I was forced to heal. Losing my grandmother really broke me. One day while visiting my mom's house, my grandmother's obituary stood out to me sitting on the dresser in her old room. Looking through the program brought tears to my eyes. On the last page there was a story from her journal. Nana would write in her journal every morning during devotion. My grandmother was rushed to the emergency room and forgot to bring her Bible. Nana had to be feeling uneasy. The nurse inquired about what was wrong with my grandmother, wondering why she was so unsettled. After expressing her frustration, the nurse went to the desk and grabbed a Bible for my grandmother to use. Nana's response inspired me the most: "When in doubt, call 91:1: 'He that dwelleth in the secret place of the most High shall abide under the shadow of the Almighty'" (Psalm. 91:1).

A relationship with God based on experience will always exceed knowing Him through the teachings of other people. Intimacy determines the capacity of the relationship. People who meet their body goals motivate others to desire that same momentum.

It's not until you become consistent with enduring the process for yourself that you are able to reap the benefits of getting the results you wish to see. My choices had to become consistent and committed to keeping myself healthy. Not only in a physical capacity, but also my mind, soul, and spirit. It was time to leave the surface and go deeper. I needed to know God for me. The One True Living God.

Knowing God for myself wasn't always my first priority. Life became challenging, leaving me feeling heavy, and forced me to lean solely on Him. Those inspirational social media posts and church just once a week wasn't fulfilling the connection I desired to have with God. Unfortunate circumstances had a way of exposing areas of my life where I lacked connection with God. Some of those challenges made me feel like I was suffocating. There are moments where you go to God willingly. Other times situations force you to fall at His feet.

I had to experience humility while my pain processed into purpose. Growth enhanced my capabilities to change pain into purpose. Being stagnant allows pain to change purpose. When I didn't understand why God would allow certain events to happen, I ran as far as space would allow. Why would my Father, the one who is supposed to love and protect me, allow life to happen in a way that left me feeling heavy? My perception of God was based on my understanding of love. My understanding of love was misaligned with the standard that Jesus Christ set on Calvary. My outlook on life conformed to the approval of this world. Which I might add, is contrary to the purpose of God. "No man can serve two masters: for either he will hate the one, and love the other; or else he will hold to the one, and despise the other. Ye cannot serve God and mammon" (Matt. 6:24).

The conditions of this world created a false perception that I once lived by which made it challenging to develop an authentic relationship with God the Father. The Bible says in 2 Corinthians 4:4 that Satan is the "god of this world." It's important to specify who you are referencing. Patterns become normalized when a large number of people are accustomed to the same characteristics. Just because a great number of people are accustomed to a certain way of living or thinking doesn't make it morally correct. I started to compare my lifestyle and thinking patterns with the standard of Jesus Christ. When I decided to know God for myself, the obstacles of life didn't persuade my perspective any longer. The standard of Christ upgraded my intellectual capacity and set the tone for every dimension in my life. The posture of my heart started to change with the way I handled conflict and challenges based on knowledge and understanding. My expectations were enlightened by the standard Jesus Christ set for me when He endured far worse pain for my sins to be forgiven. Jesus wasn't a sinner, yet He paid the penalty so humanity could have a standard on how to live.

> For God so loved the world, that he gave his only begotten Son, that whosoever believeth in him should not perish, but have everlasting life. For God sent not his Son into the world to condemn the world; but that the world through him might be saved. (John 3:16–17)

Thank you, Father God, for using me as a vessel to fulfill the plans and purpose of the kingdom of heaven. Thank you, Jesus Christ, for being the answer for mankind. Thank you, Holy Spirit, for renewing my mind, soul, and spirit. This book is dedicated to my nana, Yvonne Holt, and my Bishop, Senyo Bulla. Thank you, God, for allowing both of them to cover me.

ACKNOWLEDGEMENTS

The type of environments and experiences a person endures throughout this journey of life depicts their perception. My perception for a long time was protecting myself by any means necessary. Never giving anyone the satisfaction of being able to let me down or becoming comfortable enough to depend on another person outside of my immediate family. That became a challenge while developing my relationship with God. For the relationship to develop to its greatest capacity required me to unlearn habits and thinking patterns that blocked the relationship from growing.

Psalm 91:1 gave me a new perspective in regard to how to conduct myself in a state of emergency. It's normalized to disperse into chaos in the midst of a crisis with the intention to prevent something bad from happening. Survival instincts kick in and one has to do what's necessary to protect oneself by any means. Eventually, my experience helped me understand that God's protection supersedes my strength to overcome the power of the enemy. My job was never to protect myself. My purpose was always to posture myself at the feet of God and dwell in His presence. Correct posture expresses submission before God. Consistency develops an intimate, healthy relationship.

Psalm 91:1 was instilled in me at a young age by my mother who taught me spiritual warfare had to be destroyed in the spiritual realm. All earthly matters are considered the aftermath of what is predestined in the spiritual world. My mother made my sister and I recite this specific Bible verse every day before going off to school, but we had no understanding or revelation of what the Scripture meant. I was able to recite the Bible verse by heart. It wasn't until after I felt broken that I was able to see the Word of God manifest. "He that dwelleth in the secret place of the most High shall abide under the shadow of the Almighty" (Psa. 91:1).

To "dwell means to sit, remain, abide, or stay. During the recovery of my car accident, I was forced to sit in the house with limited mobility. Looking back on my healing process, I now see where God stripped me of my independence to teach me how to trust in Him. Dependency requires trust, something that wasn't established easily for me. Recovering for six months was about more than my physical well-being. This was an opportunity to restore my relationship with God. Circumstances weren't ideal; however, He didn't let me die in my decisions. Those that sit and remain in the presence of God are protected from everything sent to destroy them. Good posture looks like focusing on the protector, not the problem. "Abiding" is used interchangeably in Psalm 91:1. If you abide in His presence, you will abide in His power. Luke 10:19 says that, "Behold, I give unto you power to tread on serpents and scorpions, and over all the power of the enemy: and nothing shall by any means hurt you."

"Shadow" in Psalm 91:1 means "on dial and under His protection." Normally a person calls 9-1-1 at the first sight of a crisis with the certainty that help is on the way. A dispatcher collects detailed information in order to locate the person, and sends the appropriate team that will be most helpful to the situation. The dispatcher usually stays in communication until the responders are present to support the person in need. God's angels are like dispatchers in the realm of the spirit. Angels are designed to respond to the Word of God. If you have ever prayed for something and feel as though you still haven't received the answer, don't give up. Maximize your prayer life by implementing Bible verses that correspond with the results you wish to see.

TABLE OF
CONTENTS

Grab a notebook, a pen, a Holy Bible, Biblegateway. com or download the Blue Letter Bible app and follow along with the Scripture.

PART I

THE SPIRITUAL REALM: THE HEAVENS

The Mind Needs a Healthy Spirit

The power to sustain a healthy mind and spirit are keys for spiritual warfare.

"He that dwelleth in the secret place of the most High shall abide under the shadow of the Almighty."
–Psalm 91:1

I CAN DO ALL THINGS THROUGH CHRIST WHO STRENGTHENS ME

"He that dwelleth in the secret place of the most High shall abide under the shadow of the Almighty." –Psalm 91:1

Intrinsic Weapons

War or opposition usually occurs in the workplace, at home, with friends, family, or even finances. The commonality is you. There are consistent battles that surround us every day. However, the battlefield is internal. Not until my early twenties did I realize the battle starts within myself. Many years I spent time fighting the enemy in the wrong way. The spiritual world is the true battlefield for battles being fought in the natural realm. Most of my life consisted of feeling angry and expressing my feelings through fighting people. The battle felt like a never-ending cycle because I was fighting from an incorrect posture. How you respond to a crisis reflects a strong or weak prayer life.

Internal battles are often exposed through exterior circumstances. Think about the ripple effect internal battles have on your thought processing, emotions, and decision-making skills. Internal battles deny or delay the transition from who you are currently to who you were called to be. Opposing forces oppress the one who believes as an attempt to change your belief system. What was preordained for my life will be fulfilled no matter what it looks like in the physical world. "For we walk by faith, not by sight" (2 Cor. 5:7).

Intrinsic weapons regulate emotional intelligence, mental health, physical capabilities, financial stability, and spiritual capacity. Often, these types of weapons are not mentioned in schools or discussed appropriately by various mental health professionals. However, there is a mass connection with intrinsic weapons and mental health. Nothing tangible such as medication can reconceptualize the mind long term. This was the topic of discussion during a segment between Dr. Cindy Trimm and Dr. Caroline Leaf who supports the fact that "you can't medicalize misery." Mental health is the capacity to overcome stress and crisis in an effective manner. Whichever force is stronger between a problem and your mental capacity results in a state of mind. There are circumstances that destroy your peace of mind and negatively impact your physical body which can be detrimental to your mental health. It's important to develop a resistance to how situations affect your well-being. "And the peace of God, which passeth all understanding, shall keep your hearts and minds through Christ Jesus" (Phil. 4:7). Coping skills can be influenced by temptation or foundation. Cracks in my foundation left room for me to be influenced by temptation. A solid foundation builds resistance against anything that doesn't align with the standard.

In Matthew chapter 4, Jesus is being tempted by Satan after He spent forty days and forty nights in prayer with no food. This is what fasting is about. Making the flesh weak by the absence of food. Feeding your soul the Word of God empowers your spirit man to influence your mind, will, and emotions opposed to your flesh. The Holy Spirit led Jesus out of the wilderness to be tempted by the devil. Why would the Holy Spirit lead Jesus to be tempted? This thought pondered in my head for days. God's glory is revealed every time the enemy is defeated. His victory sends a message to the kingdom of darkness. After Jesus fasted for forty days and forty nights, His body became weak, but His spirit man was strong. The tempter referenced in the text uses the Word of God in an attempt to deceive Jesus Christ. The enemy wanted Jesus Christ to prove Himself by revealing His power: "Cast thyself down: for it is written, He shall give his angels charge concerning thee: and in their hands they shall bear thee up, lest at any time thou dash thy foot against a stone" (Matt. 4:6). The Scripture is referenced from Psalm 91:11. The Scripture is truth; however, the source is corrupted, which is misaligned with the character of God. One meaning of "cast down" is to let go, or to give something over to the care of another. This took place on a mountain, so it can be interpreted that Satan was telling Jesus to jump from the mountain and His angels would protect Him. Satan wanted Jesus to let go of His authority, seeing that the only way the enemy has legal rights to you is if permission is granted. Jesus Christ was consistent with dwelling in the presence of God, allowing His protection. Jesus responded, "It is written again, Thou shalt not tempt the Lord thy God" (Matt. 4:7). That was the difference with tempting Eve in the garden and Jesus in the wilderness. The knowledge of God delivers us from being bound to temptation.

Relationships reveal the truth from what's true. Eve knew God through the teachings of Adam; Jesus knew God through a relationship with Him. Jesus was able to identify the temptation because of His foundation in God. When Eve was alone and exposed to temptation, she had no personal foundation to stand on. Both circumstances give us strategies on how to defeat temptation and what it looks like to be defeated by temptation.

> Jesus Christ was consistent with dwelling in the presence of God, allowing His protection.

While studying Matthew chapter 4, the Holy Spirit revealed patterns to me. Each time before elevating to the next level of the mountain, the tempter presents an alternative option. The Holy Spirit is vital for distinguishing the plans of the enemy from God's plan for your life. After graduating from community college to a university, I was accepted to two colleges. Bowie State University, which was forty-five minutes away from home, and Delaware State University, which was three hours away from home. Around this time, I was still grieving the loss of my nana and desired a fresh start. After recovering from my car accident, I attended Bowie State University starting in 2017. Although I made the wrong choice, this situation taught me to consult God first and every good opportunity isn't a God opportunity.

Habits develop coping skills for mental health. Routines you currently have in place correlate with your mental health status. Tragic life experiences were easier to deal with buried in the back of my mind. If anyone could see some of the struggles I was facing, they would use my personal battles against me. Memories and feelings are stored away in the unconscious mind creating automatic responses like habits and behavior patterns. I had a way of moving forward from situations that remained unresolved, not fully aware how life challenges needed to be worked through in order to sustain a healthy mind, body, and spirit. Triggers have a way of exposing memories and emotions that unconsciously influence the way you think and respond to the external world.

Sigmund Freud describes three dimensions that create the structure of the mind. The structure of the mind consists of the conscious mind (aware), preconscious mind (partially aware) and the unconscious mind (unaware). The conscious mind holds our daily thoughts, feelings, and sensations. The conscious mind drives our willpower while exercising critical and logical thinking. Short- and long-term memory is also produced in the conscious mind. The preconscious mind also holds thoughts and memories. However, people are partially aware of these specific thoughts and memories, which can easily be retrieved. The unconscious mind consists of unaware thoughts and memories that become influential to behaviors and actions. Freud, along with his colleague

Breuer, utilized the "catharsis" technique to work through thoughts and memories stored away in the unconscious mind.

Dr. Cindy Trimm identified the subconscious mind and the heart as two additional components of the mind. The subconscious mind can eliminate negative self-talk and reinforce positive goals with consistency and affirmations. Your soul is the heart of your spiritual existence.

The biggest threat against mankind is ignorance: "My people are destroyed for lack of knowledge: because thou hast rejected knowledge, I will also reject thee, that thou shalt be no priest to me: seeing thou hast forgotten the law of thy God, I will also forget thy children" (Hos. 4:6). Rejecting knowledge leaves a gateway to allow the enemy to intensify the ignorance of a person and plant seeds of deception. However, the kingdom of darkness doesn't have the authority to keep you ignorant or bound. Free will was given to mankind to make a choice. God wants us to choose Him willingly. God wants you to make a lifetime commitment to carry out His plans into the world. Choosing to love someone makes the relationship more authentic.

Counsel on how to defeat both internal and external weapons is found in Psalm 91. Proactively maintaining an intimate relationship with God will shield you and give you the capacity and strength to work through unresolved circumstances. That doesn't mean only seek God when the results will benefit you. This surely doesn't mean that weapons won't try to suppress you and silence your voice. Scripture gives permission to the angels of God to fight on your behalf. The more time you spend in the Word of

God, the more you become familiar with His characteristics. Build your knowledge to identify those same characteristics in people, environments, opportunities, and even within yourself. The Bible gives a strategy to counterattack every plan outside the will of God. Who knows where I would be if I didn't get back on course. God's protection is repetitive and everlasting. Nothing can come against God. The plans of the kingdom of darkness are no match for Him. Everything orchestrating to keep you stuck in unhealthy cycles has to submit to the Word of God. You must use your voice to activate authority through Christ Jesus. Test the Spirit and see for yourself. Meditate on Psalm 91 each day. Take note of any changes, big and small. Find two to three people you can say the Bible verse with if you are open to group participation. "For where two or three are gathered together in my name, there am I in the midst of them" (Matt. 18:20).

Obstacles will continue to unfold. As you pray and digest the Word of God, remember change starts internally because the battlefield is the condition of the mind. A prayer strategy teaches you how to migrate from obstacles to opportunities. God thinks very differently than humanity. There have been times that I found myself constantly asking God to change my situation. Eventually, it seemed like the environment kept changing but the problem remained the same. The problem was me and I needed to acknowledge the internal conflict. This is what makes His Word so powerful. Many people have speculated that the Bible has been changed or altered. Have you taken time to find out what it's like to read the Word of God for yourself? The consistency of God's character is made known to humanity with hope that we can recognize His plans from our own, and the plans of Satan.

Jesus Christ transpired many obstacles into opportunities. "And, behold, they cried out, saying, What have we to do with thee, Jesus, thou Son of God? art thou come hither to torment us before the time?" (Matt. 8:29). If you continue to read chapter 8 in Matthew, you will see the demons ask Jesus to cast them into the pigs instead of destroying them for eternity. This encounter demonstrates God's character of faithfulness through Jesus Christ. Demons tormented the people in the city, which is the obstacle. This was an opportunity for God's powers to be revealed on the behalf of His people. Do you think God would be faithful enough to interfere when something or someone is trying to hinder you from getting to the season of your life? The Bible says, "And we know that all things work together for good to them that love God, to them who are the called according to his purpose" (Rom. 8:28). I knew God for many years. Since I was a child, I was committed to church. There was no growth until I became intentional about implementing biblical principles into my own life. In Matthew 17:15, there was a man seeking deliverance for his son. The father referred to the boy as a "lunatic," which is another description people use to identify severe mental health. The father of the son came to Jesus and told Him the disciples couldn't cure him. After Jesus healed the mind of the boy, the disciples inquired why it was impossible for them to cast out the demon. In verse 21, Jesus tells the disciples it is only by prayer and fasting that results in that type of authority. Prayer and fasting kills the flesh and empowers the Spirit of God to make you authoritative in the spiritual realm.

A healthy relationship involves consistency with efforts from both parties. Effort comes from the heart. What determines if something is healthy or unhealthy is based on the standard a person associates themselves with. The world tells us that magic or witchcraft has a bad and good notion. As a child, my favorite show was *The Charm Sisters*. In the show, it appeared as if the three sisters were using their powers and magic spells for good use. As I matured through my young adult years, God revealed to me that there was no such thing as good magic or witchcraft. Despite the concept that the matter may appear as if it's beneficial or even helpful, it goes against the standard that God set for humanity. Deuteronomy 18:10–12 states:

> There shall not be found among you any one that maketh his son or his daughter to pass through the fire, or that useth divination, or an observer of times, or an enchanter, or a witch. Or a charmer, or a consulter with familiar spirits, or a wizard, or a necromancer. For all that do these things are an abomination unto the Lord: and because of these abominations the Lord thy God doth drive them out from before thee.

If you are using the Blue Letter Bible app along with Scripture, you will see the title starting at verse 10 is "Spiritualism Forbidden." In your free time, read 1 Samuel 28, where King Saul consults the dead for direction. King Saul allowed the spirit of fear (another intrinsic weapon) to get a hold of him. He did in fact consult God first with how to handle the matter of what was causing him fear. Sometimes, we don't hear from God right away, which can be frustrating, or in this case, fearful. Don't allow intrinsic weapons to develop into bad thoughts and unthinkable behavior patterns.

The standard of Christ tells us that, "For God hath not given us the spirit of fear; but of power, and of love, and of a sound mind" (2 Tim. 1:7). That's my declaration until I feel peace. When I'm feeling angry, I remind myself, "Be ye angry, and sin not: let not the sun go down upon your wrath" (Eph. 4:26). There is nothing that we face or deal with in this world that God hasn't taken into consideration. How do you handle struggles? How you face challenges is based on what you feed your spirit. The Word of God reminds you to be strategic with overcoming situations or circumstances that are working against purpose. Let the Word of God inspire you to make decisions that create healthy routines and habits. The Bible is the strategy to defeat battles and overcome obstacles. Romans 12:2 says, "Be ye transformed by the renewing of your mind." Take a moment to scale your current mindset. With 10 being completely healthy and 1 being not healthy at all, how would you scale thought patterns? What determines if you have a healthy mindset or not? The Word of God is designed as a foundation to sustain a healthy mind and soul according to His standard. Take some time to think about the patterns of your thoughts and the impact thinking patterns has on your decision-making skills.

Trials and tribulations introduce people to unfortunate circumstances, setbacks, and adversity. Unfortunate circumstances are shaped in various forms to distract you from the assignment ordained over your life before birth. "Before I formed thee in the belly I knew thee; and before thou camest forth out of the womb I sanctified thee, and I ordained thee a prophet unto the nations" (Jer. 1:5). At times, what you see can distract you from what was said. Ask yourself what holds more weight—your flesh or your spirit man?

"For we walk by faith, not by sight" (2 Cor 5:7). The circumstances of life shouldn't shape our belief system. The enemy is intentional about using our ear and eye gates to conform our belief systems to normalize systems of this physical world. Belief systems are compatible with the foundation they are rooted from. The Bible is my foundation because it reminds me to stay in love with the Creator, not the creation. How you walk through life is determined by what or who is leading you. Walking with God requires faith: "Now faith is the substance of things hoped for, the evidence of things not seen" (Heb. 11:1). When first reading this Bible verse, my thoughts were to believe in things that seemed impossible to grasp. Which seemed easy, at first. My walk with God started to mature as I transitioned through life. Faith should be developed based on who God is, not solely about the capacity of my next blessing. Faith is an action.

> "For we walk by faith, not by sight" (2 Cor 5:7)

You should walk through life reliant on who can make the difference in your life. If life looks the total opposite of my prayer life, do I stop praying? This determines how big is your faith.

Walking by faith is to not be moved by the complexities of life. This doesn't negate the fact that some circumstances are difficult to deal with or recover from. My faith was tested when I witnessed God move with speed in one situation. Other circumstances, I'm still waiting for an answered prayer.

After waiting for so long, I had to ask myself, will I still have faith in God if He doesn't give me the answer I'm looking for? That is what the kingdom of darkness is all about—attempting to shake up how you think, feel, and choose God. The foundation my belief system was built upon was impactful of my choice to still walk with God even when life didn't happen the way I believed it was supposed to happen. My desire to be in the presence of God became bruised but that didn't stop me from believing.

Walking by sight is utilizing your five senses to justify how much you will believe based on what you see. At times, I ask myself if my heart is more connected to my ability to see what God can do more than my love for who He is.

You don't want to be that person who to allows life to happen to you; you want life to happen for you. The state of mind of a person is very important in a spiritual battle. Spiritual warfare attempts to cause dysfunction and confusion in the mind in order to delay and frustrate a person from persevering. Human beings operate in two realms: the spiritual and the physical world. Everything starts spiritually and forms into the natural state: "In earth, as it is in heaven" (Matt. 6:10). The competency of your mental state determines who is ultimately winning the battle. Are you conditioned by the promise or the problem? Before Jesus was resurrected from the grave, He encountered many problems. Jesus was beaten, spit on, and mistreated by His own people. No, you are not Jesus; however, His purpose was to benefit those who choose to believe. He paid the ultimate price for mankind to have another opportunity apart from sin. Sin is not acceptable in the eyes of God.

The ultimate goal for every believer is to draw people closer to God to fulfill their purpose on earth. We make up the body of Christ with the common goal of fulfilling God's plan in the earth realm through individual gifts and talents. Focus less on asking God for more and expand what He has already given you. This was my declaration for some time. Maximizing what you currently have develops good stewardship. Answered prayers are what we long for. However, how does a person contend with the blessings? The things we have currently are the fruit of what we once prayed for. How do you expand all that you have before putting your hand out for more?

Like many battles, you need armor not only to defeat the enemy at hand, but also for protection before a battle. Not metal for your physical body, but spiritual armor that protects you from deception, injustice, corruption, fiery darts from the enemy, ignorance, a reprobate mind, and prayerlessness. These weapons are considered illegal for those that believe in Christ Jesus. Illegal seeds are words implanted in your mind and heart that are not authorized to be there. Illegal seeds can form perception and habits; that is why the armor is imperative.

"No weapon that is formed against thee shall prosper; and every tongue that shall rise against thee in judgment thou shalt condemn" (Isa. 54:17). This Scripture lets me know that words are considered weapons. The Armor of God builds a standard against demonic weaponry, be it words or physical force: "Put on the whole armour of God, that ye may be able to stand against the wiles of the devil" (Eph. 6:11).

Therefore take up the whole armor of God, that you may be able to withstand in the evil day, and having done all, to stand firm. Stand therefore, having fastened on the belt of truth, and having put on the breastplate of righteousness, and, as shoes for your feet, having put on the readiness given by the gospel of peace. In all circumstances take up the shield of faith, with which you can extinguish all the flaming darts of the evil one; and take the helmet of salvation, and the sword of the Spirit, which is the word of God, praying at all times in the Spirit, with all prayer and supplication. To that end, keep alert with all perseverance, making supplication for all the saints. (Ephesians 6:13–18 ESV)

Every morning before starting my busy day, it's a priority to put on the Armor of God along with my declaration from Psalm 91, not knowing what the day may bring. The sovereignty of God triumphs over the unpredictability of life. It's important to set aside time each day to spend with God. When I don't prioritize God and put Him first, you can see it based on my interactions with other people. I'm going to feed others what I feed myself. My relationship with God is reflected in how I show up in the world.

"Thou shalt not be afraid for the terror by night; nor for the arrow that flieth by day" (Psa. 91:5). Before you go into battle, you must prepare for war. The Armor of God equips you for a fixed fight, no matter how the battle shows up. The Armor of God shields me from the arrows and devices that are seen and unseen.

"A thousand shall fall at thy side, and ten thousand at thy right hand; but it shall not come nigh thee. Only with thine eyes shalt thou behold and see the reward of the wicked" (Psa. 91:7–8). This encounter brings to mind Luke 23 when Jesus was crucified on the cross surrounded by sinners to the right and left. Jesus Christ stood in the midst of sin but wasn't consumed by it. Those that walk in Christ will inherit His disposition to overcome the wages of sin, which is death. Christ's commitment to God placed Him on the cross to die for us sinners and He never did evil in the eyes of God. He was the strategy that separated the believer from the unbeliever. The man on the right tempted Jesus to reveal Himself and come off the cross. This man allowed anger and pride to mock Jesus Christ and he died in that manner. The man to the left pleaded and prayed for Jesus to remember him. This man showed repentance and gratitude despite his circumstance. We are all sinners—which sinner represents you?

Arrows mentioned in Psalm 91 are weapons attempting to change your heart posture and silence your voice. Pastor Kevin Ewing describes the Word of God as the "Law Book." If you don't know the rules, how do you identify when your territory is being compromised?

I had to familiarize myself with the principles and laws of God. Choices we make are determined from the mindset we function from on a daily basis. You have to make a choice to be disciplined or distraction will consume you. You are either disciplined to inherit the promise or distracted by the problems and pleasures of this world. Tiphani Montgomery gave a phenomenal revelation in regard to the meaning of "dis-" in correlation with "death by distraction." This revelation influenced me to become more intentional about plucking out the root cause of why I was so easily distracted. While I was trying to fulfill my assignment in the kingdom of God, there was an assignment against me to make sure I never succeeded to endure the promises of God. There were times when I purposely distracted myself so I wouldn't have to endure the process of healing internally. When I started to be more intentional about my walk with Christ, distractions became my enemy. The way I was comfortable or familiar with dealing with my problems wasn't aligned with the path God had for me. I didn't want to submit to something I wasn't familiar with. God sends warning before destruction (see Hebrews 2:1). My warning was to be still. Something I always struggled with, God wanted to perfect. When I became obedient, God was able to deposit something. It wasn't that He couldn't fulfill His purpose while I was constantly moving. I simply needed to surrender.

Let's tap into something more worldwide, like COVID-19, for example. Not from an earthly perspective, but a more spiritual context. COVID-19 is a virus, or in biblical terms, a pestilence. Identify the significance of pestilence in the Scriptures listed below:

If I shut up heaven that there be no rain, or if I command the locusts to devour the land, or if I send pestilence among my people; If my people, which are called by my name, shall humble themselves, and pray, and seek my face, and turn from their wicked ways; then will I hear from heaven, and will forgive their sin, and will heal their land. (2 Chronicles 7:13–14, underline added)

As a nation, it appears we still have not grasped the message of what to do in a time like this. Along with COVID-19, this promise is substantial for any sickness or disease.

"Surely he shall deliver thee from the snare of the fowler, and from the noisome pestilence" (Psa. 91:3). God gave instructions and the outcome for defeating COVID-19, or any pestilence, for that matter. As I stated before, the only way to know the principles and laws of God is adhering to His Word.

Humility is a fruit of the Spirit, which is one of the characteristics of Jesus Christ. Fruits have to grow through a process in order to produce. The spirit of a believer has to go through difficult situations and circumstances to cultivate the fruits of the Spirit that replicate the character of Christ Jesus. Jesus demonstrated humility with many of His battles on earth. Jesus never allowed the decisions or other people to influence the way He handled persecution.

You know a person by their fruit. While studying the fruits of the Spirit, I noticed love was the umbrella to all characteristics of Christ. To put it in perspective, I matched all the fruits (love, joy, peace, forbearance, kindness, goodness, faithfulness, gentleness, and self-control) with encounters in the Bible that symbolize Jesus's character. Love was easy for me because it was consistently embedded in my household. It wasn't until I made a comparison to the standard of Christ that I realized my love had limitations. God loved His enemies, literally. In John 19:34–35, one of the soldiers who was a part of Jesus's crucifixion pierced Jesus's side to make sure He was dead. Blood and water was released from Jesus onto the soldier. In that moment, he grasped the understanding of Jesus's purpose. In Matthew 16:17, Simon Peter also gained understanding that Jesus is the Son of the Living God. Jesus asked the disciples, "Who do you think I am?" Based on Simon Peter's response, Jesus knew that knowledge wasn't taught by humanity. God had given a revelation to Simon Peter who Jesus is. It blew my mind how God showed that same love to the soldier who was part of killing His Son. The soldier's understanding of who Jesus Christ is demonstrates the limitless love God has for mankind. That became my new standard and outlook on love. God's love is no respecter of persons, and He is sovereign. When God has a plan for your life, He doesn't do a reference check to see if you qualify. He doesn't need approval from anyone to do anything.

Basic Instructions before Leaving Earth

We should take time to understand that the Word of God gives strategy for us to navigate through life. A pastor once presented a question during service. The question was, "Do you pray more than you read the Word?" At the time, my answer was yes. Even when I felt like I forgot how to pray, I desired a prayer life. As you mature as a believer in Christ, spiritual warfare increases. Your prayer life has to increase just as much, if not more. Defeating spiritual warfare is based on implementing the Word of God into your prayer life. To defeat warfare, you have to respond with the Word of God. Applying the Word of God in prayer derails the plans of the enemy.

Another fruit of the Spirit that represents Christ's character is faithfulness: "I can do ALL things through Christ which strengtheneth me" (Phil. 4:13, emphasis added). I can overcome any and every obstacle fashioned for my failure because God's Word is faithful. I matured to understand my physical strength wasn't going to get me far in my assignment. The more you spend time with someone, the more you take on their characteristics. When I'm feeling weak, His strength shows up as I declare His Word out of my mouth. When Jesus Christ died on the cross, and shed His blood for our sins to be forgiven, that was an act of faithfulness. God gave us strategy (Jesus Christ) to overcome anything that goes against what God already declared in His Word.

One other fruit of the Spirit is peace: "And the peace of God, which passeth all understanding, shall keep your hearts and minds through Christ Jesus" (Phil. 4:7). I was at risk of not graduating with my bachelor's degree. It was a week before graduation and my application was denied to walk across the stage. I left in the middle of my work shift and went straight to my school. I found out my teacher had given me a D in one of my core classes as my final grade. I went straight to the chairman of the department whom I knew to be the source of the matter. The chairman said I had to follow protocol and contact my teacher first before appealing the final grade. Going through the process, I noticed I wasn't upset or frustrated. I wanted to be worried, and angry about this inconvenience a few days before the big day. After I walked across the stage, I realized that unfamiliar feeling was the peace of God manifesting in my life. Even though it looked as though I wouldn't accomplish the milestone of graduation, I kept pushing and God met me on graduation day.

Lastly, this has become my favorite fruit of the Spirit after so many tests and trials—self-control: "For we wrestle not against flesh and blood, but against principalities, against powers, against the rulers of the darkness of this world, against spiritual wickedness in high places" (Eph. 6:12). For many years I struggled with maintaining self-control in the midst of conflict with others. The rates of crime have increased tremendously, highlighting violence and conflict within humanity all across the world. These catastrophes are the fruits of an unseen system at work in the spiritual realm. We have to address the system that orchestrates the times and seasons here on earth.

Feeding your spirit the Word of God is the strategy for defeating deception. The attitude of the soul sustains the mind. The posture of the heart matters because it's influential to recurring behavior patterns. Not your physical heart, but your mind, will, and emotions. Your soul is the heart of your spiritual body. God searches the heart because "the heart is deceitful above all things" (Jer. 17:9). Applying the Word of God to your life purifies the heart and re-establishes upright posture. "So God created man in his own image, in the image of God created he him; male and female created he them" (Gen. 1:27). God set a standard when He created the world of how man should conduct himself on earth. Adam and Eve had an exchange with the serpent in the garden which introduced sin into the world. God sent Jesus Christ to re-establish the standard and to cast away any deception so the believer is able to distinguish God's plans from the enemy.

"For we wrestle not against flesh and blood, but against principalities, against powers, against the rulers of the darkness of this world, against spiritual wickedness in high places" (Eph. 6:12). The fight Apostle Paul is referring to is the spiritual warfare of the kingdom of God against the kingdom of darkness. "And the great dragon was cast out, that old serpent, called the Devil, and Satan, which deceiveth the whole world: he was cast out into the earth, and his angels were cast out with him" (Rev. 12:9). The devil utilizes the systems of this world to distract mankind from the plan of God. The devil is known as the "god" of this world.

Most video games and music project violence, the love of money, sex, and drugs. Those same factors are manifested within several communities, leading to imprisonment—not only physical but spiritual bondage. This ripple effect is orchestrated by the plans of the spiritual entities Apostle Paul talks about in Ephesians.

Think of the various cities and what they are known for. Principalities have power to maximize what's already at work in a specific region. Some entities are structured and assigned to influence mankind by normalizing patterns and routines that go against God's standard.

Who or what do you allow to influence your life? The answer to that question depicts your behavior patterns and perception of life. Before a suicide attempt, depressive thoughts oppress and strip the mind of all sanity, leaving a person feeling helpless. Thoughts start to develop and run rapidly like there is nothing worth living for. Evil thoughts are arrows launched by the kingdom of darkness to misalign you from the plan God has for your life. In Jeremiah 29:11 (ESV), God says, "For I know the plans I have for you, declares the Lord, plans for welfare and not for evil, to give you a future and a hope." The Armor of God specializes in the helmet of salvation as a reinforcement to protect the mind. Things you don't kill fester and grow into something bigger. The good news is:

> Which he wrought in Christ, when he raised him from the dead, and set him at his own right hand in the heavenly places, far above all principality, and power, and might, and dominion, and every name that is named, not only in this world, but also in that which is to come. (Ephesians 1:20–21)

This is why this is a fixed fight. The new covenant of Jesus Christ defeated the plans of the kingdom of darkness for eternity. In other words, there is another level of authority you can access when you identify Jesus Christ as your Lord and Savior.

I've witnessed many people acknowledge God and only a few confess the name of Jesus Christ. Through Jesus Christ is the only way to the Father (see John 14:6). We were born into sin because of the decisions of Adam and Eve. God can't see sin. Because we were born in sin, we are considered unholy and unable to go before God until we confess with our mouth that Jesus is our Lord and Savior. It's not by my power alone that God hears my prayers. "Jesus saith unto him, I am the way, the truth, and the life: no man cometh unto the Father, but by me" (John 14:6). Being God's earthly representatives, we have access to this same authority, dominion, and power through Christ Jesus. After you have accepted Jesus Christ as your Lord and Savior, you become a part of the body of Christ.

Posturing myself correctly when praying is relevant to surrendering my plans for God's plan. Always approach God with thanksgiving first. Pray from a place of repentance with the intention to turn from sin. Lastly, make your requests known to God, for Jesus Christ intercedes on the behalf of the believer. Use the Bible as prayer-point strategies and your mouth as a weapon for the will of God to prevail in your life. You are adapting the standard of Christ where darkness has no authority.

Put into practice what we have established this far. Examine your daily thoughts for a moment. Bring every thought into alignment under the obedience of Christ. Everything that goes against what God says about you is now rejected in Jesus's name. Everyone experiences negative thoughts to some degree. Your response to negative thoughts determines how often negativity is allowed to resurface in your mind. What prompts your thoughts? Do your thoughts reflect your insecurities or your ambitions? Do the conditions of your life drive your thoughts or do your thoughts shape your reality? What you feed your mind is reflected in your thinking patterns. Despite how off course we have gotten, God still has us in mind. He sent His Son, Jesus Christ, to give humanity knowledge on how we should conduct ourselves in the world. You don't have to be ignorant if you don't want to be.

"Whatsoever ye shall bind on earth shall be bound in heaven: and whatsoever ye shall loose on earth shall be loosed in heaven" (Matt. 18:18). You have access to another level of authority and power with understanding the revelation of who Jesus Christ is. This was the declaration Jesus told Peter after his bold interpretation of who Christ is.

What are some things you need to bind and lose in your life? Declare them loudly and firmly. Take notes as needed. You eliminate the systems that are working against you, or you allow them to keep you shackled. To be set free, or to be loose, is unlocking or untying a greater version of something that was limited. "So if the Son sets you free, you will be free indeed" (John 8:36 ESV). What does freedom look like to you? Is it your finances, confidence, faith, or even your mental health? This strategy has no limitations. You bind poverty and loose wealth. Bind insecurities and loose confidence. Bind the spirit of unbelief and release faith. Bind the spirit of a reprobate mind and loose a renewed mind. Choose to think about the promises and not the problems and watch those thoughts emerge with your actions.

Legal & Illegal Seeds Implanted in Our Minds

Separate all of the thoughts that are forming in your mind into two categories. There are various ways you can become aware of your thinking patterns. Writing your thoughts down gives you a visible image. Reflecting on behavior patterns gives you insight as to what consumes your mind. Meditation with Jesus Christ refreshes your memory on what is acceptable and what isn't. Compare the fruits of your life with fruits of the Holy Spirit to determine if your thinking and behavior patterns are healthy according to the standard of Jesus Christ, and not your own. Fruits are the results of seeds that are rooted from your heart. Characteristics of God set the standard for what is not only good, but Godlike, for our well-being. Actions will follow the direction of our conversations. Your words have the capacity to shape your reality. What direction are your ideas taking you? Are your viewpoints constructive or destructive? Whether or not the thought is legal has to be compared with a standard that we live by, which is Christ Jesus. Thoughts are seeds that produce fruit, which are your decision-making skills and behavior patterns. Take some time to reflect on the fruits you are producing.

Something that is illegal doesn't have the right to exist in your life unless you give it permission to dwell. Put pressure on any illegitimate power that is current in your life. God has given us the formula to bind and cast down seeds that bear bad fruit: "Behold, I give unto you the power to tread on serpents and scorpions, and over all the power of the enemy: and nothing shall by any means hurt you" (Luke 10:19). Any deficit area in your life has to submit to the authority of Christ Jesus. You have to speak the Word of God over your circumstances and believe that what was spoken is your new reality. What was said will eventually be what you see. How much weight your prayers hold determines your waiting period for you to receive the answers to your prayers.

According to grade levels, different arithmetic and complexities of math are introduced based on the category of school age—such as elementary, middle, and high school. We eventually obtain many formulas to become successful in mathematics. There was a specific formula that helped me through school—PEMDAS. Most people are familiar with the term "Please Excuse My Dear Aunt Sally." (PEMDAS). Some people may stick to the basics: "Parentheses, Exponents, Multiplication, Division, Addition, and Subtraction." Either way, this is one of many formulas used to solve math problems with accuracy. Formulas are strategies intended to ensure you take the right steps to achieve the accurate answer.

Many people have different perceptions or views about the Bible; even I did at a point of time. My biggest disconnect from the Bible was the lack of understanding and interpretation of the mind of God. The choice of vocabulary sometimes seemed unattainable. Could it be that the English language has been normalized for many years, and conditions our mind to relate and respond only to what is familiar? That wasn't enough ammunition to keep me ignorant. "When the student is ready, the teacher will show up." "And I say unto you, Ask, and it shall be given you; seek, and ye shall find; knock, and it shall be opened unto you" (Luke 11:9).

Your relationship with God should be rooted from personal experience. Since many false prophets have emerged, 1 John 4 recommends testing the spirit to make sure it comes from God. In this generation specifically, you will identify many people who utilize biblical references and God's name for justification of their own actions. The more you read the Word of God, the more you can detect His voice and His plan more accurately. Therefore, it is wise to check the source of information, even when it's accurate. The source is just as important as the information at hand. Facts are true and God's Word is truth. Truth

> The more you read the Word of God, the more you can detect His voice and His plan more accurately.

determines if the information presented by a person or platform is in alignment or against the will of God. God gives you revelation through the Holy Spirit to understand Scripture for yourself. You can identify when someone is speaking the truth only if you yourself have an understanding of what the truth is. The Bible talks about unleavened bread, which is flat and nothing much added for ingredients. If you have ever taken communion on Sunday, that is a perfect example of what unleavened bread looks like in physical form. Leavened bread has yeast added to make it rise and more fulfilling in texture. In biblical times, the Pharisees' teaching was similar to leavened bread. Corrupted teachings that contradict the Word of God promote illegitimate belief systems for personal gain (see Matthew 16). The gift of discerning spirits confirms if what is being spoken aligns with the truth. When you have spent months, weeks, and even days being more intentional about what you feed your spirit, your appetite changes. If you try to eat something that doesn't align with your new healthy diet, your body will reject the food. When you are intentional about feeding your mind and spirit the Word of God, anything not in alignment won't have the opportunity to grow. This strategy eliminates internal confusion about what is truth and what is true. There has to be a strong foundation to determine what your mind will or will not receive concerning your growth. Corrupt teachings can compromise your belief system or misalign your walk with Christ.

Your belief system is built from a foundation. Cracks in the foundation can start to develop faulty heart posture. The influence we expose ourselves to, such as television shows, music, conversations, and family practices, are influential to our belief system.

What seeds we choose to consistently water determines what fruits are produced in the world. The next song you listen to, take note of the message behind the music. Take a reality check of what your heart is soaking up on a consistent basis. What you feed your mind shapes your perspective and outlook on life.

Let's self-reflect and identify which parable you can relate to, if any, from Matthew 13. Before we reflect, I think it's important to understand what parables are and why Jesus used them to teach the crowd of people.

Seeing that the Old Testament was originated in Hebrew and the New Testament was established in Greek, it's important to acknowledge American vocabulary has normalized a different interpretation for some words. I recently started using the Blue Letter Bible app to become knowledgeable about the Hebrew and Greek vocabulary. One of the many Greek definitions for "parable" is "an earthly story with a heavenly meaning." Mathews 13:11 informs us that Jesus Christ used parables to teach the mysteries of the kingdom of heaven.

Parable #1: Matthew 13:4: "And when he sowed, some seeds fell by the way side, and the fowls came and devoured them up."

Explanation: Matthew 13:19: "When any one heareth the word of the kingdom, and understandeth it not, then cometh the wicked one, and catcheth away that which was sown in his heart. This is he which received seed by the way side."

Parable #2: Matthew 13:5: "Some fell upon stony places, where they had not much earth: and forthwith they sprung up, because they had no deepness of earth."

Explanation: Matthew 13:20–21: "But he that received the seed into stony places, the same is he that heareth the word, and anon with joy receiveth it. Yet hath he not root in himself, but dureth for a while: for when tribulation or persecution ariseth because of the word, by and by he is offended."

Parable #3: Matthew 13:7: "And some fell among thorns; and the thorns sprung up, and choked them."

Explanation: Matthew 13:22: "He also that received seed among the thorns is he that heareth the word; and the care of this world, and the deceitfulness of riches, choke the word, and he becometh unfruitful."

Parable #4: Matthew 13:8: "But other fell into good ground, and brought forth fruit, some an hundredfold, some sixtyfold, some thirtyfold."

Explanation: Matthew 13:23: "But he that received seed into the good ground is he that heareth the word, and understandeth it; which also beareth fruit, and bringeth forth, some an hundredfold, some sixty, some thirty."

I spent hours pondering on what was the difference between each parable described in the text. Recently, I was able to identify the similarity. In verse 11, Jesus indicates that the disciples were mature with understanding His teaching without the interpretation of earthly matters. The disciples had a personal relationship with Jesus Christ; they fellowshipped with Him daily. People amongst the multitude knew Jesus from word of mouth; there was no relationship. Following Christ not only gives you authority, but also understanding of spiritual matters. In verse 15, Jesus explains why it's a struggle for many to interpret the plans of God. People's hearts are "waxed gross," which means to make stupid or callous. Fulfilling fleshly desires causes deficiencies with our spiritual senses. The Bible indicates the spirit is contrary to the flesh. You are able to sharpen your spiritual senses by implementing spiritual principles like praying and fasting.

Godlike heart posture is sustained by becoming rooted in the Word of God. The Sower, who is God, sows seeds in the heart of His people. What my heart is consumed with determines how the seed will grow and to what capacity.

According to Matthew 13, the disciples questioned Jesus because they did not understand why He spoke to the people in parables. Jesus explains that some people's hearts were hardened, making it difficult to hear from God. The disciples had the training to be knowledgeable about the mysteries of the kingdom of God by serving and taking counsel from Jesus Christ on a daily basis. The disciples weren't perfect people. However, they continued to believe in Jesus Christ and live by His standard. They were considered righteous, which set them apart from the crowd of people. People witnessed Jesus perform miracles and preach the gospel; however, they still had a hard time understanding in their hearts that Jesus really was the Son of the Living God. So, to give people a chance to understand, He spoke to them using metaphors they could comprehend. This is a characteristic of Christ I recognize to be true. God talks to me based on my level of spiritual maturity and understanding. How He speaks to me may be different from how He speaks to you. When sin was introduced into the world, it became a challenge to recognize the voice of God. Man had a fall from God making it almost impossible to communicate with Him. The birth of Jesus Christ, the crucifixion, and even God raising Him from the dead is the strategy to getting direct access back into the throne room of heaven.

The Bible teaches us to guard our hearts. Remember, the heart of your spiritual body is your soul (your mind, will, and emotions). Scary movies don't describe my idea of a good time. The main reason is not allowing fear to grip on to my heart under any circumstances. Fear doesn't always mean being scared of the dark or believing in monsters coming out of the closet. Fear can show up as sabotaging a good opportunity or relationship. Fear can keep you bound to always being comfortable. Fear has no limits or capacity. Fear is not a characteristic of God and often leads to self-destruction.

Your ability to hear, perceive, and comprehend information is determined by the condition of your heart. Your level of understanding is determined by how your heart is postured. My consistent prayer to God is to work on my heart, making me less like myself and more like Him.

When you think of a tree being planted, the strength of the root in the ground prevents a tree from falling. Depending on how deep the roots are grounded in the foundation determines the strength of the tree. Your determination to be rooted in the Word of God determines a firm posture.

Are your spiritual senses blind or deaf for any reason whatsoever? Does God utilize earthly metaphors to get your attention and ultimately improve your understanding of spiritual insight? Think of familiar patterns or moments you refer to as coincidences. You need the Holy Spirit to have unlimited access to your mind, soul, and spirit in order to understand the mystery in the matter. God uses the Holy Spirit to communicate His plans with us. "For I know the plans I have for you, declares the Lord, plans for welfare and not for evil, to give you a future and a hope" (Jer. 29:11 ESV). How can you shift your heart posture to focus on the promises instead of the problems?

CHAPTER 2

THE KEYS TO THE
KINGDOM OF HEAVEN

"I will say of the Lord, He is my refuge and my fortress: my God; in him will I trust." –Psalm 91:2

The Church I Grew Up In

Consider exactly what you were doing on September 11, 2001. Consider what the families of the victims involved in the 9/11 attacks might have been experiencing. What could individuals have been going through at the Pentagon in Arlington, Virginia, or the World Trade Center in New York City during the attack? It crossed my mind whether each person had a relationship with Jesus Christ.

I came across a video on social media that gave a tribute to the people who were scheduled to be at the World Trade Center during the 9/11 attack. For one reason or another, so many people were delayed in their day-to-day routines and for what seemed to be a bad reason. One woman was late because her alarm clock didn't go off on time. Someone else was delayed from being stuck in traffic for an extended period of time. Another woman spilled coffee on her shirt and needed time to change. This video changed my outlook on becoming frustrated and complaining when I feel like I'm running behind schedule. My father was even scheduled to be at the World Trade Center for work that day. It wasn't until my early twenties that I found out his train was delayed on the way to work. He and other passengers present on the train had to walk through the tunnel to the nearest exit.

After reflecting on the different outcomes from the tragedy of 9/11, I assured myself I wouldn't wait for another crisis to spread the gospel. A relationship with Jesus Christ is what's important. After we transition from this world, there is another life we have to attend to. Your relationship with Jesus Christ determines where you will spend eternity.

You build the kingdom of God by spreading His Word. "So then faith cometh by hearing, and hearing by the word of God" (Rom. 10:17). Something important to think about is how you affect the places and people you come into contact with. More so, think about your purpose in every experience you encounter.

How can you influence the lives of people you may never actually see? Rooms that you may never physically enter. Your relationship with Christ can influence a person or place substantially.

I was a contractor for the Department of Justice System Civil Division during my undergraduate education. My understanding of the tragic events that occurred on 9/11 had become more in depth as a result of the contract that I was briefly allocated. The contract included compensation for the victims and families that were impacted as a result of the catastrophe. To establish compensation for families, the contractors collaborated as third parties with local law firm agencies. My responsibility was checking documentation and verifying basic information. The first assignment of this experience was learning about the challenges that many people faced, including experiences that were not heard by the public through the media or another channel. Secondly, it led me to feel deeper compassion and empathy for the victims. Many of the challenges from each person's story gave me visual insight into the experiences from 9/11. People were still recovering from every angle (financially, emotionally, mentally, and physically). This was over twenty years after the traumatic experience. For me, this was a noble experience. Never having met the children or families directly didn't matter to me. The number of people I was able to influence by taking part in such a significant endeavor was the highlight of my day.

When 9/11 took place, I remember being in school along with my fourth grade classmates. Private schools were a little different from public schools. That little difference has a big impact on me, particularly on my belief system. My class prayed right away when my school learned of the tragic attack involving the airplane crashes in Arlington, Virginia, and New York City. At that moment, every class and age group, young and old, prayed with faculty and staff. "Who would like to lead the class in prayer for the victims and passengers affected by the airplane crash that took place earlier today?" Ms. Malloy posed the question to the entire fourth grade class. Delighted to have been chosen, I knelt down on my knees and joined my hands as if I were saying grace before a meal. In the classroom, the desks were arranged in a half circle. The circle was completed when Ms. Malloy took a seat at the desk behind me. I closed my eyes and started to pray. With my eyes tightly shut, I heard Ms. Malloy stand up from her seat and sit back down numerous times while I led the class in prayer. We went outside on the playground for recess after the prayer was finished. The other instructors and Ms. Malloy gathered nearby to discuss the tragic 9/11 news. Ms. Malloy expressed her amazement at my class participation: "That's a praying girl." That remark played in my head during a time in my life when it felt like I forgot how to pray. I really needed a prayer with some weight on it. Unfortunately, in that season, my prayer life had no substance.

In the fourth grade, with such a young and pure heart, I trusted God to protect and shelter the people who were involved and affected by 9/11. Twenty years later, I was reminded that prayers don't have an expiration date. The very circumstance I prayed for, God allowed me to be a part of the redemption process. "Whosoever therefore shall humble himself as this little child, the same is greatest in the kingdom of heaven" (Matt. 18:4).

God's protection from any adverse powers is invoked in Psalm 91:1–16. Not only in the spiritual realm, but also in the natural world. One of the numerous difficulties I struggled with in high school and my early twenties was anger—to the point that my future was in jeopardy. Early on, I allowed my emotions to negatively influence my decision-making skills. My mother instilled Psalm 91:1 in me every morning before school. Psalm 91:1 is a place of refuge and protection. While in contact with danger, many people reach out for help from dispatchers, such as police officers or EMT. In the world, 9-1-1 is utilized as a form of protection from various dangers. The advantage about praying in the Spirit is a person becomes privy to information and details that has not yet transpired in the earth realm. People glorify psychics, tarot card readings, and zodiac signs because the information appears to be accurate to some degree. This mediocrity is nothing to be impressed with. What's the use of obtaining information and not giving the correct strategy to war for or against it? The information may be accurate, but the source is out of alignment with the Word of God. "Jesus saith unto him, I am the way, the truth, and the life: no man cometh unto the Father, but by me" (John 14:6). Jesus Christ is the only strategy. He defeated death when He rose from the dead. Any other power outside of Jesus Christ has no authority.

> Psalm 91:1 is a place of refuge and protection.

It's a good idea to incorporate this type of discipline into your daily and overnight routines. The Word of God is good preparation. You worry less about the problem when you become proactive and consistent with becoming knowledgeable on the promises of God. The Lord is my stronghold; whom shall I fear?

Humanity represents authority in the spiritual and physical realm destined to fulfill the work of the Lord. Michael and Gabriel are among the most powerful angels I have had the privilege to recognize throughout the years. Michael is known as the warring angel who fights for God. Michael defeated Satan and banished him from heaven when Satan made a decision to challenge God. Before being cast down from heaven, Satan was also a powerful angel. His earthly deception has influenced mankind, making us ignorant to spiritual matters. Satan became jealous of God, and deceived other angels to lose their place in heaven. Once he lost his place in heaven, that was it. There is no redemption for him or the angels that followed him. This is why the enemy goes the extra mile to ensure that when he is cast into the lake of fire he is accompanied by many of God's people. "And the devil that deceived them was cast into the lake of fire and brimstone, where the beast and the false prophet are, and shall be tormented day and night for ever and ever" (Rev. 20:10).

Another well-known archangel, Gabriel, was chosen to bring good news. "And the angel answered him, 'I am Gabriel. I stand in the presence of God, and I was sent to speak to you and to bring you this good news'" (Luke 1:19 ESV). The best news of Mary's life was delivered to her by an angel. Mary became pregnant, and the angel of the Lord gave her instructions on what to name the baby.

Simply because the word "angel" is used does not necessarily mean that it is in relation to the angels of God. Several angels accompanied Satan to earth after he lost the battle in heaven.

Your Spiritual Being

After healing from my accident, school was my top priority. The numbers 911 would frequently pop up throughout the course of my day. Perhaps the time on the clock, the numbers on the road, digits on paper, or a Netflix series. Fear instantly came to mind each time my eyes focused on these specific numbers. Fear and worry might have been triggered by the significance of the number. More so, my lack of understanding the Word of God enhanced my fears. The numbers brought back thoughts of the September 11 catastrophe leading to a state of emergency. Based on my thought pattern of something happening, chaos would occur. My mind was fixated on the problems that took place on 9/11, not the promises that God endured concerning the matter. The idea that horrible things would eventually occur dreaded my mind until it became a reality. My grandmother's obituary helped me remember my posture during the 9/11 attack. The position of my hands and knees all came back to my memory.

Eventually I remembered why Psalm 91:1 was so important. "He that dwelleth in the secret place of the most High shall abide under the shadow of the Almighty" (Psa. 91:1). This was my declaration against fear. Sometimes when I ask God for something, He shows me how to establish it through a situation: "I will give you the keys of the kingdom of heaven, and whatever you bind on earth shall be bound in heaven, and whatever you loose on earth shall be loosed in heaven" (Matt. 16:19 ESV). We should recognize and learn how the spiritual realm affects the physical world. Also, how the natural realm is a reflection of everything that is preordained in the spiritual realm. Throughout this book, the goal is to increase your knowledge of spiritual warfare and adhere to the impact prayer and fasting has on your life and everything connected to you. And most of all coming to the conclusion of what a healthy life looks like to you. Not just for you and the people you love, but also for the people and circumstances you might encounter every day. The ultimate goal is drawing near to Christ and taking people with us.

CHAPTER 3

KNOWLEDGE OF A WEALTHY PLACE: IS YOUR SPIRITUAL LIFE IN THE RED?

"Surely he shall deliver thee from the snare of the fowler, and from the noisome pestilence." –Psalm 91:3

Knowledge versus Wisdom

My favorite subject in school was math, all the way until college. Learning the significance of negative and positive numbers was the best part of mathematics. It was quite fascinating to me to learn how to add and subtract positive and negative numbers. Constructing a scale while formulating the answers of adding and subtracting numbers was my favorite part. What made this so easy was visualizing a scale in my head, positive numbers moving to the right and negative numbers moving to the left. Scales can also be used effectively with therapeutic treatment. In particular, Solution-Focused Brief Therapy (SFBT) is effective. I devoted three years working for a nonprofit that focused on applying tenets of solution-focused therapy to clients we worked with on a daily basis. Clients in many organizational departments received SFBT as an intervention for improving their mental state and current behavior patterns. SFBT focuses on reconceptualizing the mind to a healthier state and developing solutions and problem-solving skills. This type of intervention helps a person to focus strictly on solutions and develop similar routines and habits that work towards a desired outcome. The reason is to transition from operating from a traumatized state of mind to a changed mindset. This technique supports individuals to disconnect from traumatic experiences and reconnect with a purposeful lifestyle. SFBT supports individuals with developing strategies to change their current circumstances.

The scaling question from SFBT gives insight on how willing a person may or may not be to work towards change. The scale inquiry gives a professional interpretation of the individual's present state of mind during the session.

Envision a scale with the phrases "healthy" and "unhealthy." Assume that you are consistent with developing healthy routines and habits that lead to success. Unhealthy routines, behaviors, and belief systems lead to destructive measures. When we are born into this world, each of us is born into sin. Salvation is accepting Jesus Christ as our Lord and Savior and becoming a new creature in the kingdom of God. What you feed your soul determines how you walk with Christ in the Spirit.

The scale depicts a person's journey by way of living. A person has a choice to walk the path of righteousness that leads to eternal life (see Proverbs 4:11). Alternative routes outside the will of God will take you to a place of unnecessary obstacles. To be righteous is the ability to still believe in Jesus Christ despite what you may come up against. Although you are walking with Jesus Christ, obstacles in life are persistent with attempting to hinder you. Maintaining healthy thoughts creates a strong mindset. Embracing healthy routines and habits produces strength despite the crisis.

Choices we make can separate us from the plan of God into eternal destruction (see 2 Thessalonians 1:9). This is considered to be unhealthy for your soul. Becoming more intentional with your choices establishes the trajectory of life.

Revelation 12 discusses how Satan departed from heaven, bringing some angels with him. The devil then established the kingdom of darkness in the world we live in today. Satan has imitated every facet of the kingdom of God. God the Father, God the Son, and God the Holy Spirit are the three members of the sovereign kingdom. Satan, the beast, and the false prophet are members of the kingdom of darkness. God uses prophets in the Bible and today's time to bring correction and warning to His people. The devil has duplicated God's work by developing false prophets who speak the Word of God with corruption (leavened bread). The plans and purposes God has for each person are detailed in the kingdom of heaven. God the Father is the Creator. Scripture gives reverence to the creation of God and how things were formed with His words. Christ Jesus is the Son of the Living God. God sent

Jesus into the world to serve as a physical manifestation of Himself. Jesus, the Son of God, preached the gospel. "Through knowledge and discernment the righteous will be rescued" (Prov. 11:9 AMP). Jesus died on the cross and shed His blood for the remission of our sins. After three days, He was risen from the dead in order to renew the covenant with humanity. As a result, you don't have to take part in formal practices as an effort to communicate with God. Jesus Christ served as a replacement to intercede on your behalf.

> God uses prophets in the Bible and today's time to bring correction and warning to His people.

Any manifestation of sin is intolerable to God. Jesus Christ bridges the gap between the world and the throne room of God. Christ is the connecting tissue between God the Father and people here on earth. The conversation with the Samaritan woman at the well in John 4:5–30 is one instance in which Jesus intercedes on behalf of humanity by impartation of knowledge. Jesus, as you recognize, enjoys a good parable. The Son of God graciously requests a drink of water from the Samaritan woman. Reading the Scripture, you can only imagine that the woman was astonished since she was a Samaritan and Jesus was a Jew. It didn't matter to Jesus where the lady came from. Jesus refers to His way of life as water that will never run dry. The time spent with the woman was intended to renew her mind and change her way of living. "God is spirit, and those who worship him must worship in spirit and truth" (John 4:24 ESV). Jesus gave the Samaritan woman knowledge on how to connect with God in the Spirit. The woman at the well knew God but her way of worship was corrupted with idolatry. Jesus Christ counterattacked the plans of the enemy by teaching her the correct way to worship and connect with God. Through the knowledge of Christ, the Samaritan woman was able to change her way of thinking and decision-making skills.

Jesus Christ was resurrected from the grave and set on the right hand of God. The Holy Spirit was reintroduced to mankind after He took His last breath on the cross.

It's important to know who or what is influential to your spirit man on a day-to-day basis. Satan couldn't be God, so he imitated God's kingdom to deceive humanity on how to live life. Studying the Word of God helps you determine which kingdom is at work in your life and the world around you.

If you never accepted Jesus Christ as your Lord and Savior, now is the time. Repeat after me, "Jesus, come into my heart and make me new. I believe you died on the cross and shed your blood so my sins can be forgiven. I believe you were risen from the grave in three days, and you defeated death by reclaiming the keys of life from the enemy. You are the Son of the Living God."

Satan created the kingdom of darkness to deceive humanity: "Having great wrath, because he knoweth that he hath but a short time" (Rev. 12:12). Satan doesn't expose himself in a way to be easily revealed. To recognize the plans of Satan, you need the gifts of the Holy Spirit found in 1 Corinthians 12. Satan is very cunning and crafty and builds his kingdom by being the ruler of this world.

Prior to Satan losing position in heaven, he was a powerful angel named Lucifer. Satan was once known as a cherubim filled with beautiful jewels and instruments. Being kicked out of heaven didn't eliminate his power of influence. Satan now uses his influence to deceive people into praising and worshiping himself and not God. Praise and worship is such a powerful ordeal in the kingdom of God. Worldly music is used to worship things of the world and to fulfill fleshly desires. The beat just doesn't sound good. There is an impartation of spiritual deception into your mind, will, and emotions. It's way beyond just having a good time. Unlawful seeds are being produced. Someone once told me sin is like a prison with an open door. You have the ability to walk away at any given time. The discouraging fact is you never know when the door will close and that chance you had to repent has passed away. There are earthly matters that are disguised with spiritual context. One of many is the world's most well-known coffee shop.

Have you ever considered looking into the image that Starbucks uses to market its products? I was initially uninterested in the logo until I had a discussion with a coworker about some of his research. My coworker had mentioned to me that the logo represents sirens and marine spirits. I executed my own study to make conclusions of my own findings. When you come across new information, it's important to have a solid foundation to make accurate judgments. Similar to looking up new terms and definitions in a dictionary. One resource I utilize as a standard to comprehend the meaning of new information is the Bible. Terry Heckler developed the Starbucks logo in 1971. Heckler did his own research on the use of sirens and marine spirits with Greek mythology books. Sirens are classified as marine spirits, which operate in the sea. Since 1971, 1987, 1992, and 2011, the logo has undergone changes to make it more pleasing to the eyes and spiritually misleading. When compared to the existing logo, the newest logo has been altered with hidden qualities and elements. This tactic keeps people from eventually asking questions or even discovering the spiritual replication of this billion-dollar company. Sirens are two-tailed creatures with beautiful voices that cause people to fall into hypnotism. Sirens are also known for ships colliding, and occasionally causing deaths. A siren's two tails represent duality. Duality is having control or influence over two realms. The original association of sirens is with the ability to hypnotize and cause accidents on ships. To be clear, all of this research I gathered from the internet. My next step is to see what instructions or examples the Bible gives about marine spirits. Over the last decade, Starbucks has become the most dominant coffee shop. Sirens are known for singing seductive hymns that would cause people to be hypnotized, leading to an early death. This is an example of the power marine spirits have underwater. I personally believe the more people purchase the coffee, the more we are giving legal access for marine spirits to have influence in the world. Offerings of money don't just work in the church. Have you ever thought about why people are so addicted to Starbucks coffee? Hypnosis causes you to operate from a reprobate mind. How does the logo correlate with people being addicted to coffee? The Bible says, "Ye cannot drink the cup of the Lord, and the cup of devils: ye cannot be partakers of the Lord's table, and of the table of devils" (1 Cor. 10:21). Forms of addiction can lead to idolatry. Idolatry is something you are committed to more than your obedience to God.

Many people believe Jezebel is a seducing lustful spirit. Despite those being some of her characteristics, Jezebel operates from a place of idol worship. Jezebel was married to King Ahab and built a temple in Samaria named Baal: "And he reared up an altar for Baal in the house of Baal, which he had built in Samaria" (1 Kgs. 16:32). The temple of Baal was created to proclaim worship to false gods. The Samaritan woman at the well participated in idol worship before she encountered Jesus Christ. Jezebel came from a family that worshiped false gods and promoted idol worship in the temple.

As I became familiar with the standard of Christ, I was able to identify things that I had begun to idolize in my personal life. Jesus gave the Samaritan woman knowledge that the way of worship they had been accustomed to was deceptive. "Thou shalt have no other gods before me" (Exod. 20:3).

In the Bible, the prophet Elijah challenged Ahab and the prophets of Baal: "And call ye on the name of your gods, and I will call on the name of the Lord: and the God that answereth by fire, let him be God. And all the people answered and said, It is well spoken" (1 Kgs. 18:24). Elijah came against 450 prophets of Baal to determine whose God was all powerful. In 1 Kings 18, the prophets of Baal prepared an altar before their god, calling out to him with no answer or response. When Elijah acknowledged the God of Abraham, Isaac, and Jacob, God answered by fire. Technology has become more and more dependable as we gradually progress through the twentieth century. Many people use social media as a platform to give prophecies and teach about God. The correlation I see with the prophet Elijah and the prophets of Baal was the ability for both sides to build altars. The disconnect I noticed was there were more prophets praying to a false god. Only one prophet prayed to the One True Living God. Though Elijah seemed outnumbered, the God of Jehovah Sabaoth was the determining factor.

Temptations or sinful attacks start as seeds in the mind. The enemy does everything in his power to move you out of the will of God. "If you are the Son of God, throw yourself down, for it is written, 'He will command his angels concerning you,' and, 'On their hands they will bear you up, lest you strike your foot against a stone'" (Matt. 4:6 ESV). Satan tempted Jesus many times while Jesus was in the wilderness fasting. The enemy tempted Jesus using the Word of God. Many can recite encounters in the Bible. The posture of the heart determines the context in which the Scripture is used.

Double-mindedness is key for recognizing the enemy is at work. "For God is not the author of confusion, but of peace, as in all churches of the saints" (1 Cor. 14:33). Feelings of inadequacies are seeds that affect your mental state. You must overcome those thoughts by empowering your soul with the Word of God. Ensure your spiritual senses are active to enhance your walk with God and resist temptation. God communicates through the Holy Spirit to his earthly representatives. The god of this world looks to lead mankind into deception. A person has to be able to stand firm on the Word of God. "Heaven and earth shall pass away, but my words shall not pass away" (Matt. 24:35).

Three Realms in Heaven

When you think of heaven, do all three dimensions come to mind? The first realm of heaven is the firmament (see Genesis 1:7–8). God divides the waters above and the waters below with a solid extended surface. The second heaven is where the plans of the enemy are orchestrated through principalities and powers of the darkness. The third realm of heaven is considered the throne room, where Christ Jesus and God the Father are seated. The structure considers rank and authority in the spiritual realm.

The conflict in the earth realm stems from unseen master spirits in high places. Think of a puppet show; it appears the characters may be walking and talking. However, there is a tiny thin line that connects the puppets to the hands of the much bigger entity behind the scenes. Puppetry is what it looks like to be influenced by the kingdom of darkness, and some people aren't consciously aware.

> God gave us authority

God gave us authority: "Behold, I give unto you the power to tread on serpents and scorpions, and over all the power of the enemy: and nothing shall by any means hurt you" (Luke 10:19). Principalities create corruption within the system of this world, such as forbidding children to talk about God in school. You need a strong prayer point to shift the educational system!

When we pray, our prayers need to ascend into the throne room of heaven. This is the case for answered prayers as well. Sometimes our blessings and breakthroughs can be withheld in the second realm of heaven due to principalities and powers of the darkness. How far will you pray to get your prayer through each dimension?

The Holy Spirit

Life is a personal journey that is created for each specific individual. "For I know the plans I have for you, declares the Lord, plans for welfare and not for evil, to give you a future and a hope" (Jer. 29:11 ESV). God already had plans for us before we were formed in our mother's womb. However, through life we are faced and challenged with free will. Following God is a choice; choosing not to follow Him is the alternative to the matter. Overall, there is a choice to be made as we journey through life. There is a choice to go left, right, or stay on the narrow straight ahead. The Holy Spirit is in sync with the mind of God. Strategize with the Holy Spirit on developing a mindset to become your most authentic self. Authenticity is in congruent with the plans God has for your life. You want to gain direct access to the mind of God to get into alignment with all that you can become. The question is, are you allowing the Holy Spirit to lead you, even without every detail?

The enemy is going to test you to figure out what standard you are living by. Connection to the body of Jesus doesn't disqualify you from being tried by the enemy. Accepting Jesus Christ as your Lord and Savior activates a covenant over your life. You now belong to the kingdom of God, and this will always be a fixed fight.

First Corinthians chapter 12 discovers nine gifts of the Spirit that are made available to God's children to expand the body of Christ. Diverse tongues are gifted through speaking in a heavenly language. On a good note, the enemy is unable to interpret what the Holy Spirit is communicating to God through you. People with the gift of diverse tongues can't often comprehend what is being said while praying. Some people have the gift of interpretation of tongues. Many have the gift of prophecy, which is different from a prophet. A prophet is a part of the fivefold ministry. "And he gave some, apostles; and some, prophets; and some, evangelists; and some, pastors and teachers; For the perfecting of the saints, for the work of the ministry, for the edifying of the body of Christ" (Eph. 4:11–12).

Knowledge is another gift of the Holy Spirit. These gifts teach the apprehension of Jesus Christ to non-believers with the ability to renew the mind. Wisdom is the gift of exercising the knowledge given to you and applying it to your personal life. Some people have the gift of faith. It's hard for the enemy to alter their belief system. Some people have the gifts of healing and miracles. Some people are gifted with the discerning of spirits to pinpoint accuracy about the plans of God. All the gifts listed above are accessible from other channels outside the will of God. This is what separates connection and corruption. "Beloved, do not believe every spirit, but test the spirits to see whether they are from God, for many false prophets have gone out into the world" (1 John 4:1 ESV).

When I first became familiar with the Holy Spirit, one of my first encounters was a thought that randomly popped into my head on my way to the car. The thought in my head was so clear it almost felt like I heard it with my physical ears. The task was simple: "Turn on your gospel station. I have a word for you." This was the perfect time to test the Spirit, so I did. A commercial was ending, and a man began to speak:

> *Your time of public revealing is coming faster than you have time to prepare for. Here's why: there are Goliaths challenging the armies of God. Goliaths like poverty, homelessness, helplessness, and prayerlessness. You have what it takes to fight the battle. When Solomon went into the city to ordain the new king, everyone was excited. Solomon examined the brothers and asked the father, "Do you have another?" The father responded, "Well, there's David." David was tending to the sheep; he was unclean, smelly, and had no time to prepare for what was happening. Solomon ordained David as the new king.*

The first time I heard this, it was shocking. After a few times of hearing the message, I realized the Holy Spirit was using this platform to speak to me.

Another time, I was flying home in the car from a friend's house. I was tired and ready to lie down. A thought popped in my head, saying, "Slow down. There will be a police car sitting near your house." As before, I took this opportunity to test the Spirit. After easing up the street, two minutes from my complex, I thought to myself, I should pray some more because there is no police car in sight. As soon as I finished my sentence, I saw the police car sitting to the right of me with the lights flashing from the car. Obedience opens new levels of understanding.

Wisdom, Strategy, & Tactics

If you had to go on a journey and you could only bring one item, what would that be and why? Take a few minutes to think about it. If I was headed on a journey and was allowed only to bring one thing with me, it would be the BIBLE.

Denzel Washington plays the main character in the film *The Book of Eli*. My interpretation of the movie is that Eli was given an assignment and encountered many obstacles along the journey. Isn't that just like life trying to hinder you from going to the next level? The instructions reassured Eli that he would be safe, provided he kept the Bible the entire way to the destination. Eli once believed that nothing or no one could stop him. The moment he released the Bible out of uncertainty, he lost his strength. In the film, Eli's adversary deceived him into forfeiting the precise thing that God had warned him about. By the time Eli arrived at his destination, he had an in-depth understanding of the entire Bible. Despite Eli's enemy having the Bible in his possession, his adversary didn't possess the keys to unlock the book. Despite the deception of the enemy, God's plan still prevails.

CHAPTER 4

STRONG PRAYER LIFE

"He shall cover thee with his feathers, and under his wings shalt thou trust: his truth shall be thy shield and buckler."
–Psalm 91:4

Prayer Is the Key

What I have learned over the years is that prayer is a posture you must maintain no matter the season of your life. Prayer seemed easy to forget when the very thing I requested manifested before my eyes. As soon as things got rocky or started to crumble, prayer was my go-to, until I forgot how to pray. When you spend so much time away from God, how to replenish the relationship seems foreign. Finding my way back to prayer started with brokenness. I had to literally crawl on my face, with tears rolling down my face with devastation. It seemed like I could pray only enough to get me through the next battle.

Prayer is like a rhythm. You should never leave your prayer closet the same way you came.

After a while, I grew to love football. I can't say I've watched a full game, or became knowledgeable about which teams have more wins and losses. When I started to understand the posture of prayer, football came to mind. What position do you play in your personal prayer life? Which type of prayer warrior are you on the battlefield—defensive or offensive? In American football, the offense team possesses the ball with the mindset to score enough points in the opponent's territory to win the game. The players of the offense team have two major positions. Offensive linemen consist of five to six team players whose primary goal is to block opponents from getting to the quarterback. There are four to five receivers that run designated routes to receive the ball, score touchdowns, and block opponents when needed. The quarterback is known as the most influential player. The progress of the team is determined based on the strong suit of the leader. For interpretation purposes, let's say you are the quarterback, or should we say, prayer warrior. Depending on the quarterback, there are different methods and tactics for studying the playbook. In this case, the playbook would be considered the Holy Bible, which is filled with various strategies

> Finding my way
> back to prayer
> started with
> brokenness.

for defeating your opponent and accomplishing the premeditated win. How well you launch the ball with boldness and confidence determines how far your prayers go and where they land on the battlefield. Seeing that the Bible is utilized as the playbook, angels that are assigned to you are commanded to move based on the Word of God. Some angels have the posture of offensive linemen. Their assignment is to block any attack coming against your prayers getting to the throne room of heaven. The Holy Spirit participates as the wide receivers in the game. The Holy Spirit is your helper, not only to ensure your prayers touchdown in a timely manner, but also to ensure that you receive the desired outcome according to the rules of the playbook.

When you become consumed with your problems, it shows up in your posture when you pray. "Behold, I give unto you the power to tread on serpents and scorpions, and over all the power of the enemy: and nothing shall by any means hurt you" (Luke 10:19). With that in mind, that changes the whole perspective of how I approach God when I pray. Prayer is a way for God to recognize your voice when you speak. The Word of God is for you to recognize His voice when He is speaking to you.

Take some time to think about what or whom you are struggling with. Now, compare that with the lifestyle God intended for you to have. Sometimes it seems impossible to look past your own personal experiences when you become mired in struggles. For instance, it may appear unattainable to achieve financial stability or even millionaire status if a person consistently struggles with money management most of their adolescence and young adult years. Measure your problems with the promises of God that are in store for you. What you focus on and prioritize the most will manifest and grow rapidly in your life. There are different postures for prayer. The first posture is thankfulness. I like to intentionally thank God through praise and worship each day. The first words in Psalm 100:1 are, "Make a joyful noise unto the Lord." That word "make" in Hebrew means to "shout in triumph over your enemies with a war." Praise and worship should be included in your posture of demonstrating continuous gratitude for who God is. Acknowledge with thanksgiving His grace and mercy that shields your life from things seen and unseen. Sometimes we get so fixated on what's going wrong, we fail to acknowledge the fixed fight of the believer in Jesus Christ.

The next posture of prayer is repentance and forgiveness. You go before God through Jesus's name because that's the only way your sins are justified. You make a declaration before God based on what He spoke in His Word. A healthy relationship with Jesus Christ is how you maintain your authority and surpass the limits of earthbound prayers.

Consider the scale you used in math class. Positive numbers are oriented opposite of the negative numbers. There is a starting point that separates both sides of the scale. Imagine yourself as the middle indication that separates the two entities. Realize that while we may choose to travel the road to a healthy life, it does not guarantee that unforeseen circumstances will not occur. "And be not conformed to this world: but be ye transformed by the renewing of your mind, that ye may prove what is that good, and acceptable, and perfect, will of God" (Rom. 12:2). There is a misalignment with the plans of God and the systematic structure of this world. God has called and chosen people not to identify with the world, but to influence the environment around us.

Learning about positive and negative numbers gave me insight on how to monitor my progress in various walks of life. Am I in a better position mentally and physically than I was three to six months ago? There is a process towards a healthy lifestyle that is not often produced overnight. Somewhere along my journey I made a lot of bad decisions, allowing my thoughts and feelings to get the best of me. At times I stumbled and backtracked. What builds my faith is knowing that at some point I wasn't certain about establishing an intimate relationship with God. Now, I can say I'm more confident with my walk with God. More certainty consists of being more vigilant about the plans God has for me. Jesus Christ is the source that helps build my faith and gives me hope. Small beginnings are often where progress begins. That little mustard seed of faith can grow as big as you would like.

CHAPTER 5

BECOMING THE BEST VERSION OF YOURSELF

"Thou shalt not be afraid for the terror by night; nor for the arrow that flieth by day." –Psalm 91:5

Me versus Me

What comes to mind when you consider who you are? Have you wondered who you could be as the most authentic version of yourself? No reference to the titles this organized world has assigned you. No need to calculate the various roles you embrace on a daily basis. Knowing who you are defines the abilities to carry out an assignment from God. If you are unsure, ask God to show you.

Affirmations constantly remind me of who I am even when I can't physically see it in myself. What are you consciously or unconsciously telling yourself? Conversations with yourself and other people are stimulated through your thoughts. Thoughts are formulated with what you feed your mind through your five senses.

What you are personally facing in the midst of a battle is key to recognizing your capabilities. The enemy attacks the place where God will maximize your strengths and abilities. The secret to discovering who you are is to familiarize yourself with the way God sees you. The beauty of trials and tribulations is the opportunity to cultivate a new version of yourself. To step into a new version of yourself requires shedding dead skin, uncomfortable growing pains, and developing faith for the unknown. Anything "new" is the elevated portion of your last season.

> What you are personally facing in the midst of a battle is key to recognizing your capabilities.

In Daniel chapter 3, the Bible talks about three Hebrew boys: Shadrach, Meshach, and Abednego. King Nebuchadnezzar had made a law that everyone under his authority would have to bow down and worship a false god which was a golden image. The three Hebrew boys knew this law was not pleasing to God and refused to abide by the declaration sent out by King Nebuchadnezzar. Anyone who refused to bow down to the golden image would be thrown in the furnace and sentenced to death. The Hebrew boys demonstrated faith in God while facing the unknown.

Their commitment to God outweighed the possibility of death. The Hebrew boys were not sure when or how God would rescue them. However, the Hebrew boys were confident that God would never leave them nor forsake them (see Deuteronomy 31:6). Because of their boldness and confidence in God, that situation changed the mindset of King Nebuchadnezzar and his belief system.

Many situations we encounter through life often feel like we are going through literal fire! Is God really with me? Is this what God really has for me? It's not until you are coming out of the fire that you recognize the Holy Spirit was with you all along. Just like the three Hebrew boys, you don't look like what you just came out of. People look at your life and wonder how it is possible for you to go through so many trials and tribulations and come out better than you went in. The fire was used to mold me and draw out any and everything God didn't ordain to be connected to me. Whether you are going into the fire or coming out, be encouraged with your walk with expectancy in your heart.

Let's find out who God says we are:

I AM THE HEAD AND NOT THE TAIL

"And the Lord shall make thee the head, and not the tail" (Deut. 28:13). A person from my executive team was critiquing me about some monthly reports I submitted in my new role as a social service coordinator. The hand gestures she used implied my work performance was at the bottom of the totem pole and the person that worked in that position prior to me was elevated way beyond my capacity. The message was clear. The Bible verse Deuteronomy

28:13 played in my head, and I repeated it over and over again until I believed what God said. If you don't become knowledgeable on how God sees you, people will try to define you based on their perspective and level of understanding.

I AM SEATED IN HEAVENLY PLACES WITH CHRIST JESUS

And God "raised us up with him and seated us with him in the heavenly places in Christ Jesus" (Eph. 2:6 ESV). Sometimes hard times and opposition make us forget the authority that was given to us through Jesus Christ. Educating yourself on the posture of Christ should give you confidence and understanding the battle you are up against has already been defeated. Use your voice to activate the authority that was given to you through Christ Jesus.

I AM MORE THAN A CONQUEROR

"No, in all these things we are more than conquerors through him who loved us" (Rom. 8:37 ESV). Don't allow the circumstances of life to depict who you are or what you are capable of. You are more than the battles you face. God is omnipotent and omnipresent. Many people including myself wonder why God would allow us to endure so much pain and suffering if He really loved us. That's an answer I don't have for you. With much practice, I try not to let the world around me dictate if God is good to me. He's been better than good to me. It's because of who He is that He is good, not what He can do for me. Before Jesus sat on the throne, He endured the cross. Jesus was mistreated and suffered past what we can think or imagine in order to save the world from sin. Everyone has to encounter the problem before the promise. The Word of God will keep you rooted and help you strategize through your battles.

CHAPTER 6

WHO AM I

"Nor for the pestilence that walketh in darkness; nor for the destruction that wasteth at noonday." –Psalm 91:6

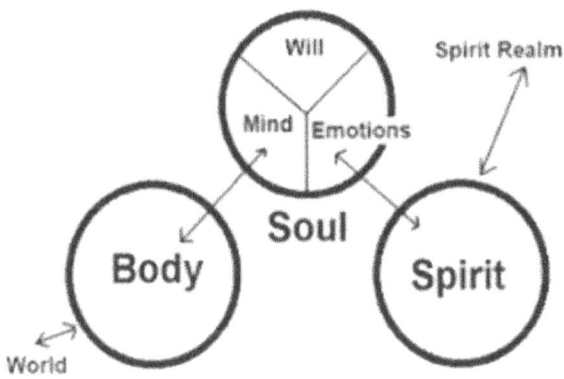

The Connecting Tissue

A ripple effect from the spiritual realm unintentionally becomes influential to the physical existence of a person. The spiritual world is like seeds having potential to grow into wheat or weeds. The decisions we make throughout life determine which seed lives and which dies. Whether you are considered wheat or weed is determined by the posture of your soul. What you feed your mind trickles down to your will and emotions. Your actions are the fruits produced based on what seeds you water the most. Are you feeding your flesh or your spirit?

The five senses have a direct influence on the capacity of your soul. Choice of entertainment and music are examples of how what you see and hear with your physical senses influences the well-being of all the components of your mind. The source of your influence determines the quality of your soul. God communicates with His people through the Holy Spirit. Unhealthy habits have a way of diminishing the ability to hear from God accurately. A close relationship with God takes consistency. Self-evaluate what factors about yourself don't align with the Word of God. The habits of others are always the focus when you don't want to spend time improving what is no longer acceptable in your own life. "And be not conformed to this world: but be ye transformed by the renewing of your mind, that ye may prove what is that good, and acceptable, and perfect, will of God" (Rom. 12:2). Because we live in a world filled with sin, it's refreshing to renew the mind daily with the Word of God.

The capacity of the soul determines the well-being of your emotions, thoughts, and will power. The mind influences the brain to take action based on the desires of your soul. If you consume healthy foods on a daily basis, not only is your body healthy but your mind becomes stronger. A person who eats fried foods, sweets, and junk food most of the day is considered unhealthy because of the effects those foods have on the well-being of the mind and physical health. Choice of entertainment and music selections are considered spiritual foods that impact your soul. People who smoke and drink are easily identified by a specific odor. People under the influence often are unaware of the smell that lingers around them while intoxicated. What we feed our spirit and body creates an unforeseen odor around people. You can always confirm the spiritual appetite of a person based on conversation, engagement with other people, and security of oneself. The appetite of your spirit defines your current mindset and emotional intelligence.

Patients who are prescribed medicine experience temporary suppression of their emotions. So, when emotions become numb, problems are not resolved—they are silenced. Emotions are also a component of the soul. If your emotions are silenced, what effect does that have on your soul? In Revelation 18:23, the Bible says the nations will be deceived by sorcery. In Greek, the word "sorcery" means *pharmakeia,* which is the use or the administration of drugs, poisoning, and magical arts. In American culture, one origin of the pharmacy is used to get prescription medication for mental health concerns. God intended to use natural healthy substances like fruits and vegetables to heal the mind and body (see Genesis 2:9).

Ask yourself what you are feeding yourself and if it is healthy according to the standard of God. If your diet is not healthy, do not worry—we will get to that in Part II of this book. Right now, the focus is to renew your mind.

"But the fruit of the Spirit is love, joy, peace, longsuffering, gentleness, goodness, faith, meekness, temperance: against such there is no law" (Gal. 5:22–23). The fruits of the Spirit represent the characteristics of Christ and the desired heart posture for a person. What you go through is not the determining factor; it's about the posture that you develop through the process that makes all the difference. The nature of your soul (mind, will, and emotions) makes the decision of how you will respond to the world through your thinking and behavior patterns. My flesh has to die in order for my spirit to produce fruits that align with the Holy Spirit.

> My flesh has to die in order for my spirit to produce fruits that align with the Holy Spirit.

The Word of God is the only thing that can silence the enemy. Measure the nature of your soul by scaling yourself according to the standard of Christ Jesus. On the right side of your notebook, list the fruits of the Spirit. On the left side of the paper, identify the fruits of the flesh.

> Now the works of the flesh are manifest, which are these; adultery, fornication, uncleanness, lasciviousness, idolatry, witchcraft, hatred, variance, emulations, wrath, strife, seditions, heresies, envyings, murders, drunkenness, revellings, and such like: of the which I tell you before, as I have also told you in time past, that

they which do such things shall not inherit the kingdom of God. (Galatians 5:19–21)

Make a mental observation of events that have occurred over the last week. Determine if your actions depicted the fruits of the Spirit or the fruits produced by the flesh. This is how you become accountable and aware of if you are walking in the right direction. Reflection leads to repentance. Actions are considered the surface of what is actually rooted in the heart. The Bible says that God looks at the heart, and above all things the heart is the most deceitful (see Jeremiah 17:9).

The biblical reference of Eve eating the forbidden fruit of knowledge of good and evil is recounted in Genesis 3. Eve introduced mankind to sin by trying to fulfill a fleshly desire. Eve was deceived by something that appeared pleasing to the physical eye which resulted in the lust of the flesh, the lust of the eye, and the pride of life. God gave Eve instructions not to eat or touch the tree in the middle of the garden. The meaning of the root word for "middle" is to cause separation or to divide. The tree in the Garden of Eden was a middle point between the flesh and the spirit. Satan told Eve that if she ate the fruit, her eyes would be open, and she would know good and evil. Desirability for things we know aren't good for us is the start of a bad cycle.

"For all that is in the world, the lust of the flesh, and the lust of the eyes, and the pride of life, is not of the Father, but is of the world" (1 John 2:16). At times it seems so difficult to live in the world as a believer. It seems harder to walk with God and easy to fall into the temptations of sin. My personal opinion—it should be the opposite. The original plan God had for humanity never included sin. However, He took what Eve did in the garden and considered us as a whole when He sent His Son, Jesus Christ, to die on the cross for our sins. The Armor of God is important with morning and night routines. Activation in the spiritual realm is a necessary part of being the best version of oneself. God bestowed upon us both power and authority. Prayer and fasting are essential for killing the flesh and strengthening your spiritual man.

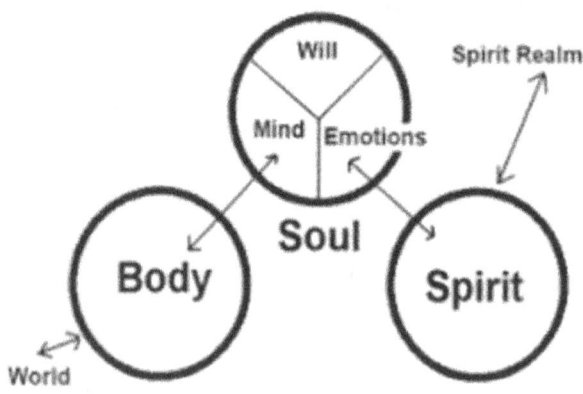

The Influencer

The soul serves as the link between the spiritual and physical realm. Your mind, will, and emotions are considered the heart of your spirit. How we approach the challenges of this world is determined by the way we are conditioned to think. Emotions are channeled through the five physical and spiritual senses. Seed develops thoughts and eventually establishes behavior patterns. "For my thoughts are not your thoughts, neither are your ways my ways, saith the Lord. For as the heavens are higher than the earth, so are my ways higher than your ways, and my thoughts than your thoughts" (Isa. 55:8–9). God has lifted a standard against fleshly desires and deception. Through prayer, fasting, and reading His Word, God can stretch your mind to surpass the standard of this world. The world projects fear while God gifts you with the spirit of faith. Counterattack the plans of the enemy by killing fleshly desires. Fasting shines light on continuous sin from generation to generation. The five natural senses are less effective while fasting. The goal of fasting is to awaken the spiritual senses and to strengthen your spirit. Fasting allows you to be led by the Holy Spirit and eliminate desires of the flesh. The Spirit opposes the flesh. Fasting consists of absence from food, and strictly feeding yourself the Word of God. Moreover, refrain from engaging in activities that take up the majority of your time. Things unrelated to God's presence are considered a consecration. Esther and Saul in the Bible fasted for three days without food or water, which is considered a dry fast (see Esther 4 and Acts 9). That's the level of fasting we should practice simply because that is the standard God set for His people. I don't believe in coincidences; I believe in revelation. The first sin was produced in the world by eating from knowledge that wasn't established by God in order to fulfill a fleshly desire. Eve thought the fruit was "pleasant to the eyes" (Gen. 3:6). Fleshly desire is not always about personal preferences; unfortunately, it's the world we were born into. To reverse the curse, we have to starve the very things that are contrary to the spirit, which is the flesh. "For the flesh lusteth against the Spirit, and the Spirit against the flesh: and these are contrary the one to the other: so that ye cannot do the things that ye would" (Gal. 5:17).

The nature of the soul has an impact on the characteristics of an individual. The nature of the soul creates motives, intentions, and habits. You have to uproot everything that doesn't align with who God says you are. What you speak is the key between heaven and earth. "Your kingdom come, your will be done, on earth as it is in heaven" (Matt. 6:10 ESV).

PART II

THE NATURAL REALM: THE EARTH

The Body Needs a Healthy Brain

Actions will follow the direction of conversations.

"For he will command his angels concerning you, to guard you in all your ways." –Psalm 91:11 (ESV)

CHAPTER 7

THE KEYS

"A thousand shall fall at thy side, and ten thousand at thy right hand; but it shall not come nigh thee." –Psalm 91:7

Authority

"And I will give unto thee the keys of the kingdom of heaven: and whatsoever thou shalt bind on earth shall be bound in heaven: and whatsoever thou shalt loose on earth shall be loosed in heaven" (Matt. 16:19). In Matthew chapter 16, Jesus taught the disciples to become aware of leavened bread from the Pharisees and Sadducees. The disciples were confused and assumed Jesus was referring to physical bread that you feed your body. Leaven is referenced to false teachings that influence the mind of a person to follow a corrupted doctrine. The foundation is faulty. The more you become familiar with the characteristics of Jesus Christ, the more you are able to accurately identify His posture through teachings and people. Being in relationship with Christ expands your intellectual capacity.

Your belief system in Jesus Christ gives you authority and dominion to bind and loose. Authority is made available to the believer through the new covenant because of the fall of man into sin at the beginning with Adam and Eve. God gave Simon Peter a revelation of who Jesus Christ was. Because of Peter's boldness of confessing the name of the Lord, Jesus Christ instilled him with the keys to the kingdom of heaven. Jesus knew based on Peter's response that this was not something that was taught to him by another person. The relationship revealed the truth. "And I say also unto thee, That thou art Peter, and upon this rock I will build my church; and the gates of hell shall not prevail against it" (Matt. 16:18). The rock represents the strength of a soul by understanding who Jesus Christ really is—the Son of the Living God. His name holds weight in each kingdom and solidifies a strong foundation. The church, which is the Body of Christ, is built based on what was revealed to Peter. Though it was revealed to Peter, the boldness of his response benefited all who believe. Hell is expected to be the maximum death sentence. Even that doesn't have enough weight to overcome the posture of Christ. Anything built on the foundation of Jesus Christ will stand firmly, down to the capacity of your spirit man. Those who confess the Son of the

> Those who confess the Son of the Living God will gain the capacity to carry the same authority.

Living God will gain the capacity to carry the same authority. Jesus Christ gave the disciples authority because of the knowledge that was imparted from God to Peter.

My declaration for 2023 was "Be Bold." Preparing for graduation, the college did some construction work to some of the buildings on campus. Walking to the field for graduation practice, there was a new slogan posted on the student center building: "BE BOLD." Sometime after, I was sitting at home having a conversation with a friend. A similar slogan was imprinted on the ginger ale can sitting on the coffee table: "BOLD." Graduation came and went; finally I got home and was able to open my gifts. There was a card from Bishop Senyo Bulla. Written at the bottom of the card was, "Be bold on purpose!"

A New Position

Preparing for a new position requires a new version of yourself, as well as learning to adapt to new beginnings, environments, and people that come along with the transition. A week or two after starting this new position, I was accommodated with a new office space. This was exciting news for me. My very own space with no limitation on my creative skills. As soon as I heard the news, I purchased a small dry-erase board to ensure engaging with my clients was meaningful and deliberate. The next day, I returned to the office with my dry-erase board and a few notebooks for my new clients. I stood at the office door, confused and a little upset that someone else's belongings were in the office that was supposed to be mine. Thankfully, the staff and owners of the agency were very welcoming and made accommodations for me. Imagine meeting someone for the first time with southern hospitality every time you meet with them. That's what it felt like working in this new atmosphere.

The front desk receptionist suggested using the conference room for my scheduled appointment. If I'm being transparent, I wasn't thrilled about the changes but was thankful for the accommodations. The conference room had a sensor light that automatically turned on when you entered the room. As soon as the lights came on, the first thing that caught my eye was the whiteboard mounted on the wall. Compared to mine, this whiteboard was way bigger than the mini board I had recently purchased. My thoughts were, "You're thinking too small." I was expecting God to bless me through a familiar process. God took me another route so I could become more reliant on Him and not the plan I was familiar with. If I didn't go into the conference room, I would have never acknowledged how small I was thinking concerning this new opportunity. With that in mind, my perspective changed. There was something bigger God had for me. The office space I thought I wanted so badly shouldn't have been my focus.

On Mondays, my clients meet me at a different location about fifteen minutes from the main office. This has been my routine for a few weeks now. This was the initial therapy session for a new client on this specific Monday. I arrived at the office thirty minutes before my appointment in preparation to meet my new client. This wasn't my first time in this particular office space at this location. However, this was my first time noticing this vast whiteboard. Now, this whiteboard is much bigger than the whiteboard in the main office. Of course, it is much bigger than the personal whiteboard I purchased from Target. The board was so big it stretched from one side of the wall to the other. The first thought that came to mind was, "Height, width, and depth." The second thing that came to mind was there were two identical boards on each side of the room. With expectancy in my heart, I knew there was a big double portion blessing coming! The opportunities God has for me are tremendous. At that time, my mind didn't have the capacity to understand how to secure these significant opportunities or where to even begin to look for them.

A few months later, the organization offered me a full-time position. My duties were to coordinate a healthy transition for incarcerated individuals back into society. This position aligned with my plan for law school. The goal was to pursue law school after completing my master's degree.

Indeed, I was excited about the position. My thesis for college focused on decreasing the negative cycles of incarcerated individuals. The research method required engaging with incarcerated individuals and utilizing the assessment tool discussed in my paper to prove my thesis. This position was right on time! The following Monday, my new supervisor held a meeting to discuss the salary for the new position. Management couldn't have done better at getting to the good stuff. "The new position pays $45,000 . . ." My instant response was, "Don't even waste your breath." I made a counteroffer of $20,000 more than the original offer. My supervisor instantly went to speak with the executive directors about my proposal. I was feeling bold and praying God would be on my side. Management came back with outstanding news. Not only did they accept the offer, but forty-five days from my start date, I would have an evaluation for another promotion. God changed my financial circumstances. Now, $60,000 may not seem like a lot to many. The knowledge I gained from that experience is not to settle and how much do I believe God is going to exceed my expectation. If God gave me a revelation that His plans for me were bigger than the plans I had for myself, why would I settle for a substitute life?

Your words are the keys to activate your authority through Christ Jesus. "And I will give unto thee the keys of the kingdom of heaven: and whatsoever thou shalt bind on earth shall be bound in heaven: and whatsoever thou shalt loose on earth shall be loosed in heaven" (Matt. 16:19).

To "bind" something means to arrest, tie together, or resist. To "be bound" is to set limits or eliminate the burden of something. To "bound" is the past tense to binding; in other words, your prayers activate heaven first and earth is the aftermath. The word "loose" is an adjective describing the state or condition of something. "Loosing" is setting something free from confinement.

> Your words are the keys to activate your authority through Christ Jesus.

When you "loose" something, it unleashes from heaven onto the earth. God gave the believer the ability to enforce His authority in the earth realm.

There was also a new position in my prayer life. God was giving me understanding of my position in the Body of Christ. Every Friday morning at 5:30 a.m., I would wake up to pray for thirty minutes with some members from my church. When the church fasted, we would meet frequently at 5:30 a.m. throughout the week. At first, the dedication seemed unrealistic. The more consistent I became with praying, the more it sustained my posture. After a few months of praying and fasting, God revealed my new position as an intercessor.

CHAPTER 8

FINANCIAL STABILITY

"Only with thine eyes shalt thou behold and see the reward of the wicked." –Psalm 91:8

I Am Wealthy

In the world we live in, money plays a significant role in how systems operate. In this generation, money comes in many forms that may encourage unhealthy habits due to a lack of knowledge and discipline. "My people are destroyed for lack of knowledge" (Hos. 4:6). One of the most common and popular forms of money people use nowadays are loans.

Baby Boomers are often caught up in "buy now and pay later" routines. This option is prevalent with many current purchases. Student loans, credit cards, clothes, shoes, and car notes are just a few examples of how this method is commonly used. However, next to various forms of money comes debt.

I was around nineteen years old when Sam's Club approved me for my first Mastercard credit card. My credit score was around 750. It was a piece of cake getting approved for everything. The max on the credit card was around $17,000. Who in their right mind would give a nineteen-year-old access to that much money? Obviously, corporate America. At that age, my focus wasn't being disciplined and knowledgeable on how to maintain a credit card. My mother always advised me to keep a good credit score and save more than I spend. I missed the part about the importance of maintaining a credit card.

Five years later, the credit card was maxed out with $398 monthly payments to be made. I had accumulated all this debt, and had absolutely nothing to show for it. In 2021, my job offered a free workshop that seemed beneficial to my financial burden. This is when reality kicked in. It wasn't until afterwards that I realized past mistakes don't have to define my future. My choices at that moment made all the difference to loosen me from this financial situation. This was my chance to turn my obstacles into opportunity.

The financial literacy workshop transformed my mindset and habits with paying off this major credit card. It took consistency with creating effective budget plans to achieve my goal of paying off the card once and for all. I spent countless hours creating adequate budgets and reorganizing my payments to expedite the process. Despite the fact that more financial resources were needed to pay off the credit card by the end of the year, that was still the deadline I created for myself. I was so tired at looking at the balance on that Navy Federal credit card. I wasn't sure where the money would come from, but I was confident and determined to achieve my goal. My confidence was stirred up from unwavering faith. I did all I could do. I prayed for God to do the rest.

Surprisingly, an opportunity showed up for me to pay the card off. My car was damaged while involved in a car accident on the highway. The insurance company compensated me with close to $17,000. The cost of the damage was 75 percent of what was paid for the car. It made more sense to consider the car a total loss. That part was easy. Just to be clear, God didn't orchestrate for me to experience a car crash. However, He considered the plan and worked it together for my good! The hard part was deciding between purchasing a new car or paying off this credit card I was extremely tired of looking at. With all transparency, the decision was challenging.

> I did all I could do. I prayed for God to do the rest.

Suddenly, I realized why paying off the card was so important. My careless habits of utilizing the card negatively impacted my credit score. Although I made payments on time every month, the balance was way beyond the 30 percent limit. A card consistently under 30 percent of the approved amount shows the person is financially disciplined and trustworthy with meeting financial obligations. My behavior patterns and bad habits with this credit card lowered my score to 650 and below. To some degree, I knew the repercussions of maxing out my credit card. The idea was pushed in the back of my mind for so long, with hope it would somehow disappear.

My prayers as of recently were to become debt free. The opportunity presented itself, and the decision was up to me. The decision I was battling with was purchasing a car or paying off the credit card.

In 2022, I paid the card off with a balance of $12,196.33. My thoughts raced back and forth about which decision was more important. I really had to write down the pros and cons for each decision. What decision was better for me at that time? Thankfully, my office and school campus were metro accessible. After I made the transfer, I felt relieved. The credit card was more damaging than going without a car temporarily. In 2024, I finally decided what car I wanted. My career was moving along, and it felt like the right time to make a good investment. I would often see the car and each time, I responded, "Thank you, Jesus." I knew the blessing was on the way. It felt like the blessing was floating right in my face. After a while I grew frustrated, wondering why I didn't have the car yet. Finally, I gained the courage to go to the dealership with my mom. The salesman brought me the paperwork for the SUV RX Lexus. Before I could read anything, the first thing that caught my attention was the number 911. I said my prayer, "He that dwelleth in the secret place of the most High shall abide under the shadow of the Almighty." I knew that was God warning me this wasn't for me at that moment. It was a great feeling to leave the parking lot with a 2021 ES 250 and no money down. What blew my mind was the ability to hear from God in the midst of the process. No, I didn't hear a voice speak with my physical ears. My mind was able to comprehend the warning of God through my spiritual senses.

Throughout this chapter, we will thoroughly discuss some techniques demonstrated to me during the financial literacy training.

LATE PAYMENTS WITH GOD

My credit card was maxed out at $17,000 with a 10.99% interest rate. The monthly payments were $398. Thanks to bi-weekly pay, $199 would go to my credit card bill every two weeks on pay day. Making minimum payments was all I could afford, but it wasn't helpful.

Now, something to always remember is any form of money that accrues interest should be paid multiple times within thirty days to see a significant difference.

The reason being is when interest is accrued, the payments are broken up into two sections. A portion of the payment pays down the interest (10.99%). The other portion of the monthly payments pay back the principle, which is the amount that was initially borrowed. The portion of the payment paid towards the interest rate is not deducted from the borrowed funds. With only two payments being made, almost $50 to $75 was taken from each payment and put toward interest. Which means my minimum payments weren't making a big difference. This was an ongoing cycle, until God gave me a new strategy.

Most people may know that it is always better to pay more than the minimum balance. Unfortunately, in this case that was the best

I could do. So, by splitting the payments up in four parts, that came to $99.50. This was my weekly routine for about a month before any changes were visible on the account. The monthly payments decreased by a few dollars each month. Later in the year, the payments decreased to $289. Little progress leads to big outcomes. The fact that this method to improve my financial circumstances was working pressured me to keep pushing. If you can pay more, that is great. If not, no worries; you will get there. Take some time to create a financial strategy for paying off any debt.

Have you missed or have any late payments with God? "Thou shalt truly tithe all the increase of thy seed, that the field bringeth forth year by year" (Deut. 14:22). Rent or mortgage payments are due at the beginning of each month to ensure you are in good standing with your landlord. Late or no payments at all create risk of being evicted and experiencing financial hardship.

In another instance, think about when you shop for clothes, accessories, new wigs, the latest shoes, or catch flights for leisure activities. Now, think about your reaction when you hear a pastor or leader of the church make a request for you to sow a seed. Paying tithes and offerings is often discussed as if it's a Ponzi scheme. At a point of time, I would give the bare minimum in church. "At least I am doing my due diligence." That was my perspective. Give five dollars here and ten dollars there. As long as I gave every week, I figured I was in good standing with God.

My biweekly income is $3,500, so my offering every two weeks should be $350 at minimum. The church is a representation of the Body of Christ. The building or location is a place for the members of the church to gather together. The people make up the Body of Christ. At a point in time, it felt like I had holes in my pocket. As if something was eating up my money. It wasn't until I abided by biblical principles concerning tithes and offering that my finances were restored. The money you have doesn't belong to you; it was given to you according to God's grace, especially if you are not a consistent giver. God is asking for 10 percent of your income and you keep 90 percent. What the leaders do with your money doesn't stop the blessings from flowing into your life. God honors principles.

SAVINGS

There are different means of saving, and distinct reasons why people do or do not save money. No matter how many bills and emergencies arise, a person should always set money to the side for themselves. Saving builds character to be disciplined and goal-driven for future endeavors. Save based on your living circumstances. For many people, such as myself, saving money was difficult for me. Often it seemed as soon as it was time to save, an emergency popped up out of nowhere, making it more difficult to save money.

Step 1: Pay God first. That may look like paying tithes in church, feeding the poor, or sowing seeds.

Step 2: Pay yourself. One hypothetical example: I get paid $1,875.67 every two weeks. At least $100 is going to my savings account every two weeks to develop discipline with paying myself first.

Another good way to pay yourself is setting up money market accounts with high APY rates. The APY rates determine how much interest is accumulated in the money market account. Most banks have specific departments to open new certificates. What if you were planning a trip or buying a house soon? Opening a money market account would be a good idea for putting money into a separate account for as short as six months. To get the best results, at least one year of dedication is needed.

Step 3: Emergency funding. Life works in mysterious ways. There are unplanned events that are always arising at the most inconvenient times. Emergency funds are always necessary. The emergency fund should be separate from a traditional savings account. Again, how often or how much a person chooses to save is totally up to that individual. Don't despise small beginnings. Discipline with finances will take someone a long way.

Step 4: Discipline your mind to allow healthy habits to become effective.

Was there ever a time you were financially stable? If so, what strategy or formula did you maintain to elevate your finances? Being content with what you have currently is the strategy for maintaining more to come. Work with what you have and expand it to its greatest capacity. Discipline develops a strong mindset and healthy habits that produce long-term results. Continue to become knowledgeable about improving financial productivity. This is healthy for the millionaire you are in the making!

MULTIPLE STREAMS OF INCOME

The average person usually has one stream of income to meet the basic needs of a household. In more fortunate cases, there are usually two incomes between two parental guardians. Having a two-parent household with two streams of income seems ideal for most.

The idea of multiple streams of income never crossed my mind until I was laid off from my job at the beginning of the year in 2023. Thank God I made the decision to pay off my credit card instead of purchasing a new car. My savings wouldn't last me long. I was uncertain of how my bills would be paid or what life would look like without having my only stream of income. This feeling of peace overcame anxiety. With certainty, I knew everything was working together for my good. My job offered me severance pay for two additional months, and unemployment resources. My first thoughts were emotional and reluctant. Being laid off seemed unpredictable and inconvenient at the time. There was literally one semester left until graduating with my master's degree. Plans had already been mapped out for my next steps after college. I felt out of breath the closer I got to the graduation finish line. Shortly after being laid off, my supervisor from my internship site connected me to another organization for possible employment. At the time, the organization wasn't hiring for full-time employment. However, there was an opportunity to accumulate hours for my internship class. At first, hearing this didn't excite me at all. My primary focus was securing employment. After a few emails back and forth, I was approved to accumulate my internship hours on site. My internship supervisor wanted to have a meeting to give me a head start on becoming acclimated with training materials. The feeling of comfortability in my current environment gave me the certainty that it was time to transition to my next assignment. Another position was offered to me to accumulate internship hours at a third site. Getting paid for an internship wasn't shocking. Three sources of income took my breath away. There was an opportunity to become trained and secure three streams of income before graduation just like I wanted. Obstacles are turned into opportunities through a process.

> The feeling of comfortability in my current environment gave me the certainty that it was time to transition to my next assignment.

CREDIT

In corporate America, credit is the gateway to many opportunities — opportunities like careers, property, cars, and so much more. The famous motto my mother used to say growing up was, "Always make sure you have good credit." Unfortunately, I missed the actual steps to maintaining what society views as good credit. It was not until my score went from 750 to 550 that reality finally kicked in. The importance of budgeting wasn't urgent until I realized the financial crisis I was creating. Credit has the ability to open doors for you or create barriers to access next-level opportunities.

There are three major credit bureaus: TransUnion, Equifax, and Experian. All debts are usually reported to one or all three major credit bureaus. Some derogatory marks that can negatively impact credit scores are past due payments, high credit card activity, and abandoned student loan payments. If you fall into one or many of these categories, RELAX—you are not alone. We are developing a strategy as you go through the process of changing obstacles into opportunities. Building up credit is not an overnight success.

Assuming when a credit card is paid off, you are finished with it for good. Unfortunately, past due payments severely dropped my credit score. The representative from the credit bureau was very generous with deleting two of five past-due payments from my account. Some footwork was still needed to break off the limitations of bad credit.

Let's try an exercise. Answer the questions below:

1. What is my credit score?

2. What would I like my credit score to be?

3. Do I have any delinquent and/or derogatory marks on my credit report?

4. Is my credit card usage under 30 percent or paid off?

Paying off debt is always better than making payments on debt. This was the lesson of the day from the financial literacy workshop offered at my previous job. At first, my monthly payments made me feel like this was a never-ending process. I established a potential goal of when the card would be paid off. Consistency was my strategy with meeting my financial goal.

Allow the answers to the questions above to be a starting point for you.

BUDGET

There were many trials and errors before I was able to budget my finances. My mother did a phenomenal job of utilizing her financial skills to teach me about money. Because I was unfamiliar with the process for myself, it was a struggle budgeting my finances. There are seasons of abundance and seasons of famine. Create routines and habits that can balance your harvest. In Genesis chapters 40 and 41, Egypt experienced seven years of harvest and seven years of famine. God gave Joseph a strategy to preserve food for the seven years of famine from the plentiful harvest. Financial discipline creates wealth. Managing small portions develops healthy habits for bigger portions.

Budgeting is a healthy tactic for providing financial longevity. Budgets should be reevaluated frequently to enhance healthy financial habits. Re-evaluate the last time you updated your budget. Utilize the workbook or personal journals to strategize a new budget. List the total amount of your monthly income. Divide your budget into four categories: GOD, monthly bills, debt, and savings. Set a goal for yourself starting with six or twelve months. This will allow you to track your progress of becoming disciplined with what you already have.

CHAPTER 9

WHAT ARE MY STRUGGLES?

"Because thou hast made the Lord, which is my refuge, even the most High, thy habitation." –Psalm 91:9

The Solution

The biggest struggle for me was separating from who I was and becoming who I am supposed to be. Becoming the most authentic version of myself seemed like a long shot from where I was standing. Past experiences shape the perspective of the present, and imprint footsteps for future endeavors. Each day you should evolve internally and allow external platforms to execute your growth. Life has trials and tribulations that can expand you to a limitless capacity. Struggles aren't identified as such until they start negatively influencing your life. In other cases, struggles can be disguised as intrinsic blind spots or external barriers. Everyone has faced struggles at one point in life. There are people like myself that struggle with transitioning from a comfortable place to something more challenging. Breaking and building habits can be a struggle.

Struggles have a way of making people become comfortable and complacent. Sometimes we create struggles for ourselves based on patterns and perspective. I measured my success based on dates and time stamps. I struggled with letting go of my plan and allowing God's plan to propel in my life. One of my greatest skills is being organized. Planning is my strategy for being organized. Seeing that I wasn't privy to the plans of God, there wasn't much for me to map out.

To struggle with something is a mindset. The definition of struggle is to make <u>forceful</u> or violent attempts to break free of <u>restraint</u> or <u>confinement</u>. Sometimes the fight is beyond physical strength. The real things we wrestle with are structured to fatigue the mind and exhaust the body. "For we wrestle not against flesh and blood, but against principalities, against powers, against the rulers of the darkness of this world, against spiritual wickedness in high places" (Eph. 6:12). The things we struggle with are not of this world. Because of what Jesus Christ did on Calvary, there will always be demonic systems that fight the believers. The systems are wrestling to see if pressure will

> The real things we wrestle with are structured to fatigue the mind and exhaust the body.

change your mind about God. Over time I enjoyed a little tussle. Difficult situations had a way of expanding my prayer life. "Put on the whole armour of God, that ye may be able to stand against the wiles of the devil" (Eph. 6:11). "Wherefore take unto you the whole armour of God, that ye may be able to withstand in the evil day, and having done all, to stand" (Eph. 6:13).

The Armor of God consists of the belt of truth, the breastplate of righteousness, the shoes of the gospel of peace, the shield of faith, the helmet of salvation, and the sword of the Spirit. In verse 11, after putting on the Armor of God, you will have the power or state of mind to influence situations and circumstances of this world. Situations and circumstances don't have enough power to influence or dictate your life. There are expectations and agendas of how each day will play out, but we aren't always certain. The armor equips you to sustain the authority that was given to you. You become immovable. One of the many definitions for "to stand" is to escape to safety. The definition brought me to Psalm 91:1. A vivid image of a safe place in God.

Verse 13 indicates to use your armor during the battle. You will have a state of mind to resist anything attacking your physical and mental wellbeing. Your struggles will be used to strengthen a greater version of you. Say it with me: my struggles are my new strategy. This battle is a fixed fight.

The Armor of God represents the strength and power of God. The first instruction was to put the armor on. The second instruction says to press up against the standard that sets you apart. The strength of God now separates you from the struggle while strengthening you in the process.

Strategy as the Swiss Army Knife

Becoming knowledgeable about a Swiss army knife gave me insight on how the Body of Christ operates. The original purpose of this unique tool was intended for soldiers to open up canned foods and dismantle weapons. Originating from the same foundation with similar purpose, the Body of Christ consists of believers who are faced with battles every day. Each person is gifted with a unique ability to defeat the enemy. The foods to strengthen unique gifts and talents are sealed in the Word of God. Feeding yourself the Word of God strengthens you to dismantle the attacks of the enemy. "For the word of God is quick, and powerful, and sharper than any two-edged sword, piercing even to the dividing asunder of soul and spirit, and of the joints and marrow, and is a discerner of the thoughts and intents of the heart" (Heb. 4:12). The Word of God is a standard that is precise with segregating the mind, will, and emotions of a person that is insufficient to the Holy Spirit. The standard dictates whether the foods you eat are healthy or a hindrance to your gifts and talents. The standard measures your capacity to deactivate the plans of the enemy using God's strategy and not your own.

> Each person is gifted with a unique ability to defeat the enemy.

The mental health clinician at my previous job described me as a "Swiss army knife" in relation to my work performance. Not so familiar with the terminology, however, the compliment made me feel good. My coworker went in depth to explain the correlation of characteristics between me and the Swiss army knife. Later that day, I did my own research to discover the Swiss army knife is a strategic weapon equipped with multiple tools. Though the Swiss army knife and the Bible have similar characteristics, the Word of God is sharper and cuts deeper than any blade you see promoted in this book.

Before we come to a solution for a problem, we must strategically plan on the most effective outcomes. We all encounter various struggles, very different, sometimes very similar. Actions will follow the direction of conversations. You can utilize Biblegateway. com or the Blue Letter Bible app to find the Scripture based on your personal circumstances. My suggestion is to study the Kings James Version (KJV) to advance and challenge your intellect. In the search bar, describe the type of Scriptures you need for reference. The Blue Letter Bible app is intended to give you context of the Scripture from its original language. The Old Testament originated in Hebrew and the New Testament originated in Greek. Digging a little deeper can give you the understanding you need.

CHAPTER 10

EMOTIONAL SUPPORT

"There shall no evil befall thee, neither shall any plague come nigh thy dwelling." – Psalm 91:10

A Strong Support System

Take a moment to think about morning routines. Are you only recognizing capabilities in one realm and blind to the other?

The condition of the mind is systematic to routines and patterns. The mind is subject to the brain. The thoughts allowed to surface through the mind manifest behavior patterns and words in response to the circumstances of life. The words we choose to speak predict the course of life: "Death and life are in the power of the tongue: and they that love it shall eat the fruit thereof" (Prov. 18:21).

God's Word is often foreseen as support throughout the various transitions in life. What you engage with on a consistent basis is a representation of the current support system you have in place. Your activities measure where you spend the majority of your time. God was working on me to change up my routines and habits. As I started to mature, the conviction settled in that I spend too much time looking to the world for support and not God.

What foods you eat impact the structure of the brain. It's one thing to be conscious of activities that are clearly not good for you. It's another thing to be blinded by unhealthy desires based on too much consumption. The body needs a healthy brain to function effectively. Keeping the body healthy is centered around how well you take care of your internal self. It's like a ripple effect. Sometimes people use unhealthy foods as emotional support. My emotional support at a point in time was soul food. For some people, like myself, the sound of food brings joy to my heart. The type of foods you eat determine the well-being of your physical body. When you adopt bad eating habits, it often shows up in your skin, your weight, and even health conditions. What you feed your soul influences the perspective of your mind, will, and emotions—even "foods" like music, television shows, social media, and consistent routines. You can't physically see what is being transferred to your soul. The transference is conditioned through thoughts and actions. Either the Holy Spirit or an opposing spirit is influencing your thoughts, will, and emotions. The Holy Spirit has given us gifts to make proper judgment of what we allow to enter our ear and eye gates. The Holy Spirit was made available to the believer after Jesus died on the cross. The gifts of the Spirit give us insight on the way we should live according to God's Word (see 1 Corinthians 12:8–10).

· · · CHAPTER 11 · · ·

MENTAL
HEALTH STATUS

"For he shall give his angels charge over thee, to keep thee in all thy ways." –Psalm 91:11

Maintaining Mental Health

W ithin weeks of starting my new job, the executive directors invited me to a meeting focused around neuro-feedback. The purpose of the meeting was to make observations and evaluate the four frequencies found in the brain. With little to no knowledge of what they were talking about, the more we discussed it, the more the information became intriguing to me. Alpha brain waves relate to creativity and daydreaming usually in a relaxed mood. Beta waves are produced in the middle of deep thinking or problem solving. Delta waves can be increased during deep sleep. Theta waves produce deeper problem-solving skills through sleep. There was a scale with positive and negative numbers demonstrating the activity or frequencies from my brain.

The negative numbers represented a need of support for enhancing specific areas of the brain. The positive numbers represented an inhibited condition. There was a need to decrease frequency in the self-conscious state. Meaning, there was too much activity in certain areas. Think about areas in your life that you have mastered. You have exceeded the expectations in specific domains of life. Continuing to thrive in places where you are successful is far from a bad thing. If you choose to take time to grow or improve in unfamiliar territory, you develop a balance. The health profile summarized five components of measuring activity in the brain: Frontal, Central, Posterior, Timing Index, and Focus Index.

This intervention gave a visual image of how much a person utilizes their brain and to what extent. Improvements can be implemented based on the results from the assessment. The results of the evaluations were compared to other people all over the world in the same age bracket. The assessment was able to examine how lifetime experiences affect the frequency of the brain and to what capacity.

There are various sections throughout the test. The sections consist of questions and a meditation component. The last part of the evaluation consists of games. All this was prompted through an app downloaded on my phone. My first thought after seeing the results was the one area that needed improvement. The entire team assured me the results from the assessment were outstanding. Areas of improvement included the need for more sleep to increase theta waves throughout the brain. When I feel unsettled, it's hard for me to sleep at night. The testing seemed to be accurate. One trivial piece of information that stuck with me from the assessment was the task performance. Reaction time was scored as medium. My responses throughout the test weren't very speedy. My ability to focus generated accurate results despite not performing rapidly. The question remains, how can my expertise support me in areas that need improvement?

It's not just about what we eat, but what is "eating us." Dr. Cindy Trimm pinpointed this during a segment entitled "An Open Heaven and Healed Mind." Foods we eat on a consistent basis have the ability to restore or damage the brain. The results from the assessments gave me another perspective with regard to transitions throughout my life. Thoughts are turned into actions through neuro pathways that exist in the brain. Unhealthy habits like food and thinking patterns cause brain damage by limiting the physical ability to maximize all components of the brain. The mind takes what is digested in the mind and develops actions through the brain. Your soul doesn't have

> The question remains, how can my expertise support me in areas that need improvement?

an expiration date like your physical body. The posture of your mind is determined by the attitude of the heart. Your soul is the heart of your body. God sent Jesus Christ to bring deliverance to the soul. "And be not conformed to this world: but be ye transformed by the renewing of your mind, that ye may prove what is that good, and acceptable, and perfect, will of God" (Rom. 12:2). Being in a certain environment or around the same type of people for long periods of time makes you likely to adapt patterns within your environment. We are born into sin, so that is primarily the first instinct. God sent Jesus Christ as a standard to humanity of what it looks like to be transformed. Your physical body submits to your mindset. Adapting the mind of Christ is healthy because He is the light that drives out darkness. The Word of God teaches what is right and wrong according to the standard of God. In reading the Word of God, your body begins to reject conformity to the systems of this world.

In 2019, I worked as an intake specialist for a non-profit organization supporting children and families with community resources. Six months later, I started case management under a CFSA contract as a case manager. Solution-Focused Based Therapy (SFBT) was one of the most challenging yet unique ways to engage clients. Challenging because traumas had a way of resurfacing if not worked through effectively. Unresolved issues could potentially be exposed through the professional relationship with my client. In therapeutic relationships, transference is the ability for clients to project their feelings and emotions onto the clinician. Countertransference is the nature of the clinician to project unresolved traumas onto the client. The inability to work through traumatic experiences negatively influences mental health status.

One of my favorite tenants from SFBT is the scaling question. The scaling question can be used to recognize progress and target points. The well-being of your mental health is vital for proceeding from one phase of life to the next. An unhealthy or abandoned mental state can hinder physical and cognitive performance. Sometimes there is residue leftover from various transitions through life. Reconceptualize the way you respond to uncomfortable changes. If you are forced to carry weight, it can be interpreted in two ways. This pressure is going to break me, or this weight is going to make me stronger. Freud and a colleague named Breuer demonstrated working through problems with a technique called "catharsis." In Greek, "catharsis" means to purify or to cleanse. Fasting from foods and feeding yourself the Word of God allows for God to purify your internal and external existence. Freud's theories described three dimensions of the mind. The conscious, preconscious, and unconscious mind. Freud's theory also supported the idea that emotions, memories, and thoughts stored in the unconscious mind have an impact on perspective and behavior patterns. Catharsis is utilized to bring all thoughts and feelings to the conscious mind while simply talking through problems and challenges. Catharsis can be practiced in many forms. Think of unsettled situations as dirty toxins that block or decontaminate moments of healing to move forward in life.

Another component that is most enjoyable about SFBT is focusing completely on the solution at hand. It's important to identify the problem, yes. Problem-solving skills should be the focus. Start changing what you allow your mind to focus on.

The mindset in which you function empowers the brain to make decisions. The nature of the soul influences decision-making skills.

Fruits for the Spirit versus the Lust of the Flesh

Eve ate the fruit from the tree of the knowledge of good and evil. Her actions exposed mankind to the lust of flesh, the lust of the eye, and the pride of life. This was a gateway for the enemy to start a battle with humanity.

Satan uses fleshly desires as a gateway to corrupt mankind. The Holy Spirit equips a person to become familiar with the standard of Christ so you can accurately discern correction from corruption. Both strategies are intended to influence the mind and behaviors of people.

It's a worldwide tradition to eat fruits and vegetables to keep the brain and body healthy. Seeing that the brain is subject to the mind, it's important to keep your mind and spirit in good shape. "But the fruit of the Spirit is love, joy, peace, longsuffering, gentleness, goodness, faith, meekness, temperance: against such there is no law" (Gal. 5:22–23). The more you draw closer to God, the more you inherit His posture. Your actions will reflect the heart posture of God opposed to your own. Something that I constantly pray is that the Lord works on my heart, making me less like myself and more like Him, in Jesus's name. Fruits that are produced are a reflection of not what you are eating, but what's "eating you."

The lust of the flesh is the desire to prioritize physical need. It has absolutely nothing to do with the will of God. There is a desire for temporary physical pleasure. Fulfilling physical desires is one component of conforming to the systems of this world. When the physical need is prioritized, this opens the door for layers of temptation. Idol worship is a result of conforming to the ways of the world.

Jezebel operated from a spirit of idol worship. The primary focus is directed to the matter and not the maker. Idol worship goes against the laws of the Lord given to Moses (see Exodus 20).

First Kings chapter 19 talks about the account with Jezebel fighting against the prophet Elijah. Jezebel represents a strong principality or master spirit that enforced Baal worship to the world. Dependency on horoscopes to predict what the future holds is considered idol worship. Often when I meet new people, they ask, "What's your sign?" That's a false standard people have become familiar with which develops a false perspective. Accurate information is true, but Jesus Christ is truth. Is the standard in correlation with the foundation of God? "Thou shalt have no other gods before me" (Exod. 20:3).

Perspective of what is considered healthy or unhealthy varies depending on the person. Perspective is a way of thinking based on the condition of your mind. By what standard do you measure your thoughts and patterns?

We Walk by Faith, NOT the Lust of the Eye

"Now faith is the substance of things hoped for, the evidence of things not seen" (Heb. 11:1). Faith is believing in something you can't see with your natural eye. Faith requires discipline to wait for God's promises to prevail in your life and not settle for alternative motives depicted with the natural eye. Faith comes by hearing the Word of God which makes you knowledgeable. Faithfulness is a characteristic and also a gift of the Holy Spirit. Faith is understanding the truth of who God is by character. Jesus remained faithful to the plans of God until death.

The lust of the eye desires fulfillment from earthy matters. Eve ate the fruit from the tree of the knowledge of good and evil with the mindset that it would make her wiser. Eve thought she could benefit more from something she could see with the natural eye in conflict with the instructions given from someone she could not see.

> Faith comes by hearing the Word of God which makes you knowledgeable.

This reminds me of deception with fortune tellers, psychics, tarot cards, and zodiac signs. These rituals are assumed to give a person knowledge regarding the future or current circumstances. In some cases, I hear the information could be accurate. However, if the source of the knowledge goes against the standard of Christ, the information is considered unfruitful. The absence of Christ Jesus is unfulfilling. Rituals of this sort ascend in the spiritual realm through other spiritual channels outside the Holy Spirit. This is a very popular tactic, yet misleading. What separates true from truth is understanding the capacity of Jesus Christ. Operating in the spiritual world from any channel is powerful. Jesus's name gives authority to make every opposing spirit the footstool of Jesus Christ.

Financial gain is a major discrepancy in various parts of the world. Money is also a major resource that drives the structure of the economic system. Having money isn't always bad. An avarice mindset gives wealth a false perception. Desperation is the gateway to being deceived.

Judas's desire for money led to the betrayal of Jesus Christ. Judas's love for money led to acts of betrayal. He did the unthinkable for thirty pieces of silver. The love of money produces bad fruit. What the heart is attached to determines if the outcome will be substantial or not.

A Pure Heart versus the Pride of Life

During my transition from one job to the next, God humbled my heart. Exodus 14:14 (ESV) says, "The Lord will fight for you, and you have only to be silent." My perspective at that time was when someone did me wrong, God would make them suffer on my behalf. As time went on, I noticed there were no drastic changes, at least for me to see. There will be encounters where God will exceed you and pass the places and people who hurt you. Those environments and people will be in good standings to see the strength of God through your life. God's strength elevates you to the next level. I was distracting myself with the past, focusing on the downfall of my adversaries. Similar to walking backwards. Eventually you will crash if you are focused on what is now behind you. My heart needed to be purified.

A purified heart is being able to practice the characteristics of Christ even when it seems like an inconvenience to your own plans. To be humble is the ability to sustain the fruits of the Spirit when it's not easy, and not to allow the battles of life to change your heart posture. Posture your heart to overcome the battle. Reflect back to when Christ was crucified. Jesus was spit on, beat, and treated with malicious intent. Yet He was postured in long-suffering in obedience to God's will and love for humanity.

No pain is greater than the affliction Jesus endured for my and your sins to be forgiven and hearts to be purified. Life has a way of sometimes making me feel like I'm drowning at times. It can be something unexpected or a prolonged process that seems never-ending. Compared to the pain Christ endured, it changes my perspective every time. The level of understanding changes your weight. The same strength was given to the one who believes Jesus is the Son of the Living God. He is Lord.

Matthew 27 talks about when Jesus was crucified. During my childhood, watching the film *The Passion of the Christ* gave a visual of Jesus's crucifixion. There was a point in my life where I became overwhelmed. Seemed like chaos was in every direction. In the middle of the movie, the feeling of burden went away. Knowing what Jesus did on the cross is exceptional. Understanding what Jesus endured and why He did it makes me feel at fault for murmuring and complaining.

Actions Will Follow the Direction of Conversations

Dreams are never too far-fetched. The process to endure the vision causes an elevated version of who you are currently.

Before you became the first millionaire in your family, you thought of a plan to make that possible. Before graduating from college or trade school, you had to set your mind to believe, "I can do this!" Before the book became successful, I had to think of ideas and techniques to enhance my abilities to become dedicated. Before you launch that business, you plan according to your expectations. Every behavior starts as a thought. There is a process to turn the seed into a harvest. What does your process look like? When farmers prepare for a harvest, they start the process months in advance. What does preparation look like to you?

At some point there is mental preparation required in order to shift. When you come to the conclusion something needs to change, you develop a mindset to make that happen. Be honest with yourself about yourself—out loud. Make the plan and prepare your mind for the process.

Using the five questions below, identify the following:

Who do you talk to when you first wake up and when you go to bed at night?

What do you spend most of your time talking about in conversations?

When you listen to music and/or watch television, is it expressing healthy or unhealthy connotations in the message?

Where do you spend most of your time?

How can you contend with healthy habits?

The reason I became convicted about complaining was the understanding that what I could see was only a portion of what was happening. I'm not always privy to every detail considering the plans of God. The possibility of me speaking against the process God has for me wasn't worth losing access to the promise.

Driving in the car on my way home, this heaviness pressed down on my back. I asked God at that moment why I felt so weighty. That pressure on my back represented the process I had to go through.

It's your choice of perspective that determines your capabilities for whatever you set your mind to. Don't allow the perspective of others to determine how a situation will unfold. Perspective is built on experience. Unfortunately, there are many people who feel inadequate based on what they remind themselves of everyday. Experience has a way of shaping reality. It should be the Word of God that shapes the way we think. My experience is not your experience, and vice versa. Any experience is what you make of it. Everything you mastered you once learned, and everything you are learning you will eventually master, as long as you are intentional about what you feed your mind. Your mindset determines what actions are feasible, and what actions are too far-fetched.

Let's focus on a long-term goal. Over the next ten years, where do you want to be in life? If you need assistance, use your short-term goals (five years or less) to identify where these short-term goals will lead you. You can never be too detailed about the expectations you have for your own life!

The first question to ask yourself is, how healthy is your diet? What foods do you consume daily? This is very important to the productivity of the human body, especially when you are enhancing your abilities to achieve more. After you think about your goals, utilize the five "W" questions below to help narrow down choices and future opportunities. Start with your short-term goals to ensure you are on the right track to fulfill long-term goals in due course. I will complete one exercise with you:

(Two should be completed in total, for short- & long-term goals.)

Who can mentor and/or counsel you to assist with fulfilling your goals?

What skills do you need to achieve your goals?

When do you plan to complete your goals?

Where should your mental health status be to finish your goals strong?

Why are these goals important to you?

Instead of focusing ahead, look up. Meaning, instead of focusing on how bad circumstances seem, focus on health possibilities that can transform through your relationship with God. It's time to take control of your thoughts, not thoughts taking control of you. The second step after acknowledging the problem is realizing it's time to shift. Shift the direction of conversations and actions will follow.

Words of Affirmation

Growing up in my mother's house, we often practiced words of affirmation. As a child I did not realize the significance of this small gesture and how it would benefit discovering my identity. Words of affirmation bridged any gaps of confidence. Many people are familiar with the love language "words of affirmation." Words of affirmation are positive phrases used to build up confidence, self-esteem, and overall, a positive mental health status. This specific love language is not limited to a relationship with a spouse. During my internship for school, I would meet with families on a weekly basis. Each family participated in a creative activity identifying individual love languages. The purpose of the activity was to identify how each person perceives love. If you take time to understand another person's perception of love, that itself can strengthen the relationship.

> If you take time to understand another person's perception of love, that itself can strengthen the relationship.

Words of affirmation seem like a small gesture. Those gestures feed your mind healthy reminders in order to sustain different transitions through life. What you feed your mind, you feed other people. It's a ripple effect. Your mind should be able to reject unhealthy thoughts before they become patterns because of the declaration you tell yourself on a consistent basis.

Words of affirmation create a foundation for who you are beyond titles and roles filled on a daily basis. If those titles changed, does that change who you are? Self-talk is another means of producing healthy habits. Ensuring who you are gives an idea of what you are capable of.

· · · *CHAPTER 12* · · ·

THE SOUL IS THE CONNECTING TISSUE

"They shall bear thee up in their hands, lest thou dash thy foot against a stone. Thou shalt tread upon the lion and adder: the young lion and the dragon shalt thou trample under feet. Because he hath set his love upon me, therefore will I deliver him: I will set him on high, because he hath known my name. He shall call upon me, and I will answer him: I will be with him in trouble; I will deliver him, and honor him. With long life will I satisfy him, and shew him my salvation." –Psalm 91:12–16

To "imbrue" means to stain the spirit and taint the soul. Your soul is the foundation of your thoughts, your will, and your emotions in which you function on a day-to-day basis. The capacity of your soul determines the standard in which you live. The soul formulates posture and attitude.

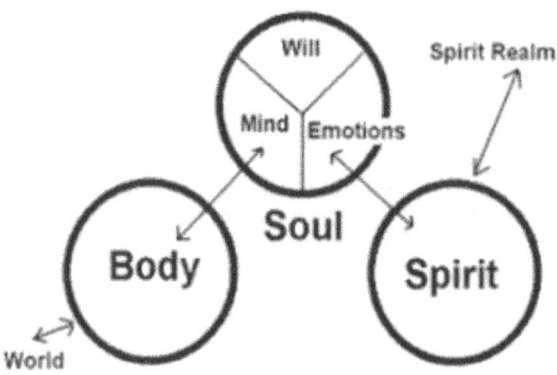

My mom teaches a Bible class every Monday. During the first class, we talked about establishing a healthy foundation. My mom used the structure of a building as a metaphor to explain the importance of a solid foundation. If the foundation is solid, everything built on it will be steady and grounded. Your soul is the foundation of your existence. Actions and recurring patterns are rooted from your mind, will, and emotions. The capacity of your emotional intelligence is determined by the nature of your soul.

Think of the result of eating unhealthy food. Now think about when you have patterns of a healthy diet. The mind and body feels more energetic and nourished with eating fruits and vegetables. Feeding your spirit using your ear and eye gates measures the soul and influences behavior patterns. The capacity of your soul influences perspective and how you respond to people and situations.

Everyone is familiar with what a corrupted soul looks like. Your mind is unable to function in a healthy state. What matters are the means to close any doors that contribute to an unhealthy lifestyle.

Fasting is a means to change the condition of your soul from unhealthy to healthy. Fasting is a pattern of feeding your mind, will, and emotions the Word of God. Tiphani Montgomery has a corporate fast the first three days of every month. The fast takes place from 6 a.m. to 6 p.m. From 6 p.m. to 6 a.m., those who participate are able to eat raw fruits and vegetables only. This type of fasting reminds me of what many people know as the Daniel fast. Not only did Daniel eat raw fruits and vegetables for his physical health, but also to posture his soul in order to hear accurately from God. In Daniel chapter 2, King Nebuchadnezzar had a dream that the magicians, the enchanters, and the sorcerers were unable to explain. The interpretation of the king's dream was given to Daniel from God after fasting and praying. Fasting and praying has a way of shutting down your physical senses and gives the ability to hear accurately from God. Daniel was confident in his ability to hear from God because of the relationship that developed.

When you run water over a sponge consistently, eventually it gets heavy. It's not until you squeeze out the water absorbed in the sponge that it becomes light again. The soul soaks up everything it's exposed to. It's the heart of your body. Seeds are sown into the heart based on what you see and hear. Seeds grow into behavior patterns based on the consistency to feed what was planted. Everything you do starts in seed form. The fruits produced give you confirmation if the seed was healthy or not.

In John 4:14 (ESV), Jesus encounters a Samaritan woman at the well. Jesus said, "But whoever drinks of the water that I will give him will never be thirsty again. The water that I will give him will become in him a spring of water welling up to eternal life."

The woman was unfamiliar with what water Jesus was referring to. Her mindset was focused on the physical water that nourishes the body. When you are accustomed to feeding your body, your soul lacks maturity to comprehend spiritual matters. In verse 25, the woman stated she knew of Jesus but had no relationship with Him. The Samaritan woman was adamant about figuring out what water Jesus was talking about.

But the hour cometh, and now is, when the true worshippers shall worship the Father in spirit and in truth: for the Father seeketh such to worship him. God is a Spirit: and they that worship him must worship him in spirit and in truth. (John 4:23–24)

Jesus gave the Samaritan woman wisdom about how to connect with God in truth. Declaring the Word of God through prayer enforces His will into earth. The Samaritan woman knew of God. Her means to connect with God was outside of His Word. Jesus gave the woman a strategy that pieced together the cracks in her foundation. Everything that exists in the natural realm was predestined in the spiritual realm. "Before I formed thee in the belly I knew thee; and before thou camest forth out of the womb I sanctified thee, and I ordained thee a prophet unto the nations" (Jer. 1:5). Prayers ascend into the spiritual realm with the intentions to bind or loose. The Word of God makes your prayer life effective.

This is why medicine doesn't cure the mind. The condition of your spirit and functions of the mind are based on the foundation of your soul. In Daniel chapter 4, a warning was given to King Nebuchadnezzar that he was dealing with the spirit of pride and he needed to repent. Again, Daniel was able to interpret the dream for King Nebuchadnezzar and confirm the warning from God. King Nebuchadnezzar's failure to take heed of the warning from God led to him losing his mind for a short time.

The generation we live in correlates pride with the LGBT community. Pride is a condition of the heart which desensitizes the need for God. Over time, morals and typical behavior have shifted, allowing room for misinterpretation. God's standard doesn't shift or change for anyone. Pride is a posture towards God. This is not celebratory to a group of people.

The diagram at the beginning of this chapter represents the correlation between this physical realm and the spiritual realm. The commonality between the two is access to your soul through your ear and eye gates. The spiritual world communicates with your mind through your soul. Each dimension of the mind determines how your brain and body operate.

The battlefield is in the mind over the standard of the soul. If the world can defeat you in your mind, you lose control of your actions.

This is why it's important to pray and ask God to give the Holy Spirit unrestricted access to your mind, soul, and spirit. The kingdom of God is a heavenly place and considered a spiritual matter. The Holy Spirit is a part of the Trinity, or sovereign kingdom: God the Father, God the Son, and God the Holy Spirit. The spiritual realm is broad, however. The Holy Spirit gives you direct access to the mind and characteristics of God. "But the fruit of the Spirit is love, joy, peace, longsuffering, gentleness, goodness, faith, meekness, temperance: against such there is no law" (Gal. 5:22–23).

The Holy Spirit cleanses the soul and renews the mind to desire the things of God and not of this world. The fruits of the Spirit give insight of the type of attributes your spirit can produce.

The systems of this world are corrupted by the plans and schemes of the enemy. Nowadays, the educational system is attempting to forbid any students from talking about God while at school. Imagine how that decision has impacted the mindset and behavior patterns of the next generation.

Hospitals and ambulance trucks were my biggest fears growing up. The red sirens on the truck and the smell of the hospitals made me think the worst of the worst. This is how my brain was programmed for years. My nana visited the hospital often growing up. Now I understand my initial fear as a child was witnessing my grandmother being transported to the hospital in the ambulance truck. Pain and fear I felt during those moments was associated with the bright red lights and the scent from the ICU. Those memories replayed in my head until my adult years.

My mom needed me to pick my youngest sister up from the hospital and take her home. Going to the hospital, fearful of the smell and the condition of my grandmother, I left as fast as I could. My hope was to be as quick as possible with the intention that I would see my grandmother at home in a few days as usual. The first person I saw was my nana, and instantly I walked away with tears in my eyes. Conflicted was the best way to describe it. A part of me wanted to hug and kiss her, and the other part of me couldn't bear to see my baby hurt and there was nothing I could do. The spirit of fear had taken over my thoughts and influenced my behavior patterns every time I went to the hospital.

A short time after, my mother woke my sister and I out of our sleep to say our goodbyes. By this time, my grandmother was not responsive. My grandmother couldn't verbally speak, but she could hear everything we said, according to the doctors. To me, this still wasn't enough. Not the person who helped raise me. The women I admired and loved with all my heart. I didn't get a chance to say a sincere goodbye due to being fearful of what might happen. The very thing I was fearful of happened anyway. Not only did my person leave me, but my last encounter did not go as planned. The passing of my nana imbrued the posture of my heart. My pain quickly turned to anger, ultimately with God. My heart hurt and I blamed God for taking my nana from me and not preparing me to say goodbye beforehand. So, I left the state. Anything familiar reminded me of my nana. This was drowning me.

In August of 2016, I attended Delaware State University for a short period of time. It seemed like the right thing to do at the time. A fresh start seemed appropriate at the time. I wanted to start over in an unfamiliar environment where I wasn't constantly reminded of the unsettled pain from my nana's passing. If you are still wondering—yes, I was still angry with God. The words couldn't part from my lips, but feelings of anger and unforgiveness surfaced in my heart. I let my relationship with God fall to the wayside.

A month after being on the waitlist, the leasing office approved me for my first apartment in Delaware. The decor was already picked and paid for; I was more than excited to move into my first apartment. A day after moving in, a car crash happened on the way back home to Maryland. It took me some time to realize it was me who had been involved in the T-bone car accident. Being in a coma for three days, it took me some time to remember my birthday, social security number, and other vital information. I remember thinking, how is it I'm waking up in the very place I feared the most? It reminds me of the story of Jonah in Jonah chapters 1 and 2. Jonah was fearful and decided to run from God and spent three days and three nights inside the belly of a fish.

The first thing that came to mind was the test in my 10 a.m. class and the first day of my new job. Everything was making me anxious. My mom let me know that the injuries from the car crash were severe and there was no chance of leaving the hospital anytime soon. My ribs and pelvis were fractured, making it impossible to walk. The memory that is most vivid to this day was everyone in the ICU clapping and cheering me on as my mom closely watched me use the walker to take my first steps since the car accident. There was a hematoma in the back of my skull which caused internal bleeding, which was one reason why the ambulance medevacked me to Christiana Care Hospital. Suddenly, I remembered an encounter on the helicopter prior to waking up in the hospital bed across from my mom. I'm unsure if this encounter should be classified as a dream or vision. However, the experience was spiritual, if anything.

The sound of the helicopter woke me out of my sleep. My body was in so much pain, the first thing that came to mind was something bad happened. Leaning over to the left, my body felt so heavy. Every attempt to sit up straight was painful. The pilot turned their head around slowly and made eye contact with me. The pilot's face was an imitation of my grandmother. The exciting feeling quickly went away after the pilot slowly turned their head and made eye contact with me for a second time. This time with a sly grin, and haughty eyes. Fear gripped my shoulders; something felt wrong. Why would the sight of my grandmother project fear onto me?

The imitation of my grandmother had two meanings behind it. My nana was the very reason why I distanced myself away from God. Unforgiveness and anger settled in my heart after her passing. The second revelation that God helped me understand was that the condition of my heart allowed the enemy to gain access in my life. "Be ye angry, and sin not: let not the sun go down upon your wrath: Neither give place to the devil" (Eph. 4:26–27). Unforgiveness and pride festered in my heart, shutting down all communication with God. There wasn't an explanation good enough for me.

The condition of your soul is what God plans to purify and the devil plans to corrupt. There are behavior patterns within society that are considered right or wrong, either by politics or individual perspective.

Psalm 91

He that dwelleth in the secret place of the most High shall abide under the shadow of the Almighty.

I will say of the Lord, He is my refuge and my fortress: my God; in him will I trust.

³ Surely he shall deliver thee from the snare of the fowler, and from the noisome pestilence.

⁴ He shall cover thee with his feathers, and under his wings shalt thou trust: his truth shall be thy shield and buckler.

⁵ Thou shalt not be afraid for the terror by night; nor for the arrow that flieth by day;

⁶ Nor for the pestilence that walketh in darkness; nor for the destruction that wasteth at noonday.

⁷ A thousand shall fall at thy side, and ten thousand at thy right hand; but it shall not come nigh thee.

⁸ Only with thine eyes shalt thou behold and see the reward of the wicked.

⁹ Because thou hast made the Lord, which is my refuge, even the most High, thy habitation;

¹⁰ There shall no evil befall thee, neither shall any plague come nigh thy dwelling.

¹¹ For he shall give his angels charge over thee, to keep thee in all thy ways.

¹² They shall bear thee up in their hands, lest thou dash thy foot against a stone.

¹³ Thou shalt tread upon the lion and adder: the young lion and the dragon shalt thou trample under feet.

[14] Because he hath set his love upon me, therefore will I deliver him: I will set him on high, because he hath known my name.

[15] He shall call upon me, and I will answer him: I will be with him in trouble; I will deliver him, and honour him.

[16] With long life will I satisfy him and show him my salvation.

Help me get the word out about the message of this book...

- Post a 5-Star review on Amazon.

- Write about the book on your Facebook, Twitter, Instagram, LinkedIn, – any social media you regularly use!

- If you blog, consider referencing the book, or publishing an excerpt from the book with a link back to my website. You have my permission to do this as long as you provide proper credit and backlinks.

- Recommend the book to friends – word-of-mouth is still the most effective form of advertising.

- Purchase additional copies to give away as gifts.

The best way to connect is by visiting:

prettywomenthatprayfoundation.org

You can order these books from

or wherever you purchase your favorite books.

www.ingramcontent.com/pod-product-compliance
Lightning Source LLC
Chambersburg PA
CBHW061805120626
46550CB00005B/2149